March 2012

Thanks for Supporting the <u>Greatest</u> <u>Race</u> in The World!

Brebeuf "74"

How Much Do You Really Know About the Indianapolis 500?

500+ Multiple-Choice Questions to Educate and Test Your Knowledge of the Hundred-Year History

PAT KENNEDY

authorHOUSE®

AuthorHouse™
1663 Liberty Drive
Bloomington, IN 47403
www.authorhouse.com
Phone: 1-800-839-8640

www.autoracingtrivia.com

First published by AuthorHouse 3/25/2011

ISBN: 978-1-4490-8896-5 (e)
ISBN: 978-1-4490-8894-1 (sc)

Library of Congress Control Number: 2010904369

Printed in the United States of America
Bloomington, Indiana

This book is printed on acid-free paper.

FOREWORD

I am honored to be asked by Pat Kennedy to write a few words of introduction for his book of "500" trivia questions.

As I have expressed on other occasions, to me the ideal trivia question is one in which a person either is able to provide the correct answer after a certain amount of mental taxation or, at the very least, they should be delighted upon learning the answer. Among the happiest and most satisfying sounds I know of are those of a human voice exclaiming variations of "Really? No kidding? I didn't know that!"

Although I am fascinated by a variety of subjects—and my wife and I have a long-standing nightly ritual of watching "Jeopardy"—the Indianapolis 500 has always been "it" for me. Ever since I first learned about the "500" as an English schoolboy, and the floodgates of information subsequently burst open, it has been the source of a bottomless treasure trove of trivia.

Among my true delights—once I had arrived at the Speedway and been blessed with the opportunity of becoming "involved"—has been to create a trivia question, ask it of a driver and, after they have been unable to determine the correct answer, gently reveal that the correct answer was them!

I have no idea what first attracted me to the "500," but I do know that the names of the drivers and the cars definitely had something to do with it. Even as a 14-year-old, I knew that

Kennedy Tank Specials had run in the "500" in the 1930s and '40s. When I finally achieved a longtime ambition by arriving at the track as a young adult in 1964, I was privileged to encounter literally hundreds of people I had read about and seen pictures of in Floyd Clymer's priceless Indianapolis 500 yearbooks. Among the first people I met were Bill Kennedy and "Big John" Berry, whom I later found out had married into the Kennedy family.

After I moved to Indianapolis the following year and became employed by the United States Auto Club, I was a guest for several years at a May function put on at the Speedway Motel by a group called The Purchasing Agents. John Berry was one of the organizers. Typically, the featured guests would be six or eight journeyman "500" drivers (who would be paid the princely sum of $25 each) and I would help with the introductions. It was a different world back then, and it was always an enjoyable evening.

In more recent years I have come to know Bill Kennedy's son Pat, and I am delighted that even after all these decades, not only is the Kennedy Tank Company still alive and prospering, but it is still family-owned. Not only that, but Pat likes "500" trivia. It was probably the spring of 2009 when he first told me he had been working on preparing a quiz with which he hoped to do something. I believe he had 25 or 30 questions at the time.

Every time I would run into him at the track during May, his idea had become a little more grandiose. Thirty questions became 50, and then 100, then 200 and so on, the end result being a book containing 581 questions!

Pat elected to go with "multiple choice," and just as there is a whole art to phrasing a trivia question, a multiple-choice quiz can be made harder or easier merely by the potential answers listed. I would rate Pat's questions generally as a pretty fair challenge because in most cases none of his four options is easily to be dispensed with as being particularly outlandish.

So sit back on your own, or get together with your friends, and prepare yourself for a challenge.

Donald Davidson

Historian

Indianapolis Motor Speedway

March 2010

Joie Chitwood, grandfather of the former president of the Indianapolis Motor Speedway (Joie Chitwood III), in 1940. Joie Chitwood drove the Kennedy Tank Special to a 15th place finish. Second from the left, behind the car and moving right, are William E. Kennedy Jr., William E. Kennedy Sr. and John M. Berry.

Dedication

Dedicated to my dad, William E. Kennedy Jr.; my great uncle, Big John Berry; and my grandpa, William E. Kennedy Sr.

Their passion for, interest in, and love for the Indianapolis 500 and IndyCar racing was instilled in me at a very young age and continues strong to this day.

Special thanks to Angie Brackin, my right hand on this project, whose interest and commitment made this project possible.

Many thanks to Donald Davidson, the savant of the Indianapolis 500, whose support and guidance were critical in completing this project.

Thanks to everyone involved in this book from the Indianapolis Motor Speedway for their helpful assistance.

Lastly, special thanks to Mark T. Watson, my life long best friend, whose artistic talent designed the book cover. Spotlight Photography-(317) 894-3666

Contents

About the Book

Test your knowledge while educating yourself on the greatest automobile race in the world. For 100 years, the greatest spectacle in racing plays out each May in Indianapolis.

The entire scope of the Indianapolis 500 is presented in this fun test: drivers, track information, teams, race information, cars, rules, records, and so on. Challenge yourself with the new Green/White/Checker chapter especially for "500" experts.

Grade your knowledge on the Indy 500 scale. The answers are provided in the back of the book.

Good Luck!

www.autoracingtrivia.com

Chapter 1
Drivers

1.   Salt Walther raced in seven "500s." What was his real first name?

(a) Anthony
(b) David
(c) Herschel
(d) Thomas

2.   Rick Mears drove at the Speedway for how many years before crashing a car?

(a) three years
(b) seven years
(c) 11 years
(d) 14 years

3.   Which winner became the first since Ray Harroun to retire in Victory Lane?

(a) Jimmy Bryan
(b) Sam Hanks
(c) Johnny Rutherford
(d) Al Unser Sr.

4. What was Jim Clark's occupation prior to becoming a race driver?

    (a) airplane pilot
    (b) engineer
    (c) mechanic
    (d) sheep farmer

5. Who was the first African American driver to qualify at Indy?

    (a) Carmelo Anthony
    (b) George Mack
    (c) Walter Payton
    (d) Willy T. Ribbs

6. In 2005, defending champion Buddy Rice had an accident in practice that resulted in a broken back, preventing him from defending his championship. Which former winner, who was also recuperating from serious injuries, took over his car, actually qualifying with the fastest qualifying speed?

    (a) Kenny Brack
    (b) Eddie Cheever
    (c) Buddy Lazier
    (d) Arie Luyendyk

7. The 1939 pole sitter Jimmy Snyder was a former what from Chicago?

    (a) airplane pilot
    (b) mailman
    (c) milkman
    (d) truck driver

8.   Between 1930 and 1932, this top-notch driver led 410 of the 421 laps he completed, or more than 97 percent. Who was this driver?

(a) Billy Arnold
(b) Fred Frame
(c) Louis Meyer
(d) Louis Schneider

9.   Which potential race favorite was injured in a motorcycle accident in the infield on Pole Day 1969 and was forced to miss the race due to a broken ankle?

(a) Roger McCluskey
(b) Johnny Rutherford
(c) Al Unser
(d) Bobby Unser

10. The pole winner in 2001 did not make it past the first turn on lap one before getting in a single-car accident. Who was it?

(a) Scott Goodyear
(b) Roberto Guerrero
(c) Greg Ray
(d) Scott Sharp

11. Name the driver who arrived at the Speedway in May of 1966 with both arms in casts from a sprint-car accident at Eldora that prevented him from competing at Indy?

    (a) Ronnie Duman
    (b) Billy Foster
    (c) Bobby Grim
    (d) Johnny Rutherford

12. Whose car was Tony Bettenhausen testing in 1961 when a suspension failure caused the car to barrel-roll flip down the main straight, proving fatal for Bettenhausen?

    (a) Eddie Johnson
    (b) Eddie Russo
    (c) Paul Russo
    (d) Shorty Templeman

13. Match the driver with his hometown.

Rick Mears	(a) Bakersfield, CA
Bobby Rahal	(b) Dayton, OH
Danny Sullivan	(c) Louisville, KY
Salt Walther	(d) Maui Island, HI
Danny Ongais	(e) Medina, OH

14. In 2000, there were for the first time, two female drivers in the field. Who were they?

    (a) Sarah Fisher
    (b) Danica Patrick
    (c) Lyn St. James
    (d) Desiré Wilson

15. What was the hometown of 2000 pole sitter Greg Ray?

(a) Dallas, TX
(b) Fort Worth, TX
(c) Houston, TX
(d) Plano, TX

16. What driver is famous for the "spin and win" in 1985?

(a) Michael Andretti
(b) Rick Mears
(c) Bobby Rahal
(d) Danny Sullivan

17. Which driver is remembered for spectacular flips down the main straight in three successive years in the early 1960s, resulting in his retirement from racing?

(a) Bob Christie
(b) Allen Crowe
(c) A. J. Shepherd
(d) Jack Turner

18. What former winner had four fine finishes in his first four "500s"—second, second, first, and second?

(a) A. J. Foyt
(b) Bill Holland
(c) Tom Sneva
(d) Rodger Ward

19. Who was the first Mexican driver to qualify for the Indy 500?

(a) Josele Garza
(b) Roberto Guerrero
(c) Bernard Jourdain
(d) Pedro Rodriguez

20. Bob Harkey drove in six "500s." Besides racing, what was another occupation?

(a) bar owner
(b) insurance salesman
(c) stuntman
(d) tax collector

21. What "500" winner wore a green shamrock on his helmet?

(a) Billy Arnold
(b) Jimmy Bryan
(c) Pat Flaherty
(d) Jimmy Murphy

22. In 2004, the son of a former winner qualified for the first time in a car using the same paint scheme and car number as his father's winning car. Who was it?

(a) Marco Andretti
(b) Larry Foyt
(c) P. J. Jones
(d) Robby Unser

23. Who was Mario Andretti's twin brother?

    (a) Aldo Andretti
    (b) Jeff Andretti
    (c) Marco Andretti
    (d) Michael Andretti

24. The winner of the first race of the Hulman era in 1946 was George Robson. In what country was he born?

    (a) Canada
    (b) England
    (c) Germany
    (d) USA

25. After eight years of trying, which driver finally qualified for the race in 1976 and finished 25th?

    (a) Sheldon Kinser
    (b) Ralph Liguori
    (c) Al Loquasto
    (d) Jan Opperman

26. Which racing brothers swapped identities (first names), to get around age restrictions so both could race, and retained those identities for the rest of their lives?

    (a) Mears
    (b) Rathmanns
    (c) Unsers
    (d) Whittingtons

27. Which driver won the pole position then was fatally injured in a practice accident the next week?

   (a) Tony Bettenhausen
   (b) Scott Brayton
   (c) Floyd Roberts
   (d) Bill Vukovich Sr.

28. What was the birth place of Mario Andretti?

   (a) Nazareth, PA
   (b) Rome, Italy
   (c) Speedway, IN
   (d) Trieste, Italy

29. Which of the following winners was the only one who never failed to qualify for the "500" race when they made a four lap qualification attempt?

   (a) Emerson Fittipaldi
   (b) A. J. Foyt
   (c) Buddy Lazier
   (d) Bobby Rahal
   (e) Johnny Rutherford
   (f) Tom Sneva
   (g) Al Unser Jr.
   (h) Rodger Ward

30. Who was the first Japanese driver to qualify for the "500"?

   (a) Kosuke Matsuura
   (b) Hideshi Matsuda
   (c) Hiro Matsushita
   (d) Tora Takagi

31. Who was the first third-generation starter in the "500" whose grandfather and father also competed?

    (a) Marco Andretti
    (b) Al Unser Jr.
    (c) Robby Unser
    (d) Bill Vukovich III

32. Who was the first driver to win the "500" for Roger Penske?

    (a) Gary Bettenhausen
    (b) Mark Donohue
    (c) Rick Mears
    (d) Al Unser

33. Sammy Sessions raced in seven Indy 500s. What city was he from?

    (a) Nashville, IN
    (b) Nashville, MI
    (c) Nashville, TN

34. What former three-time American Motorcycle Association National Champion came within a whisker (nine laps) of winning the "500" in 1968?

    (a) Arnie Knepper
    (b) Joe Leonard
    (c) Jochen Rindt
    (d) Sammy Sessions

35. Who was the second African American driver to race at Indy?

    (a) Spike Gelhausen
    (b) Dee Jones
    (c) George Mack
    (d) Lee Roy Yarborough

36. Which "500" winner was largely responsible for Jack Brabham deciding to compete in the Indianapolis 500 in 1961?

    (a) Jim Clark
    (b) A. J. Foyt
    (c) Graham Hill
    (d) Rodger Ward

37. Didier Theys raced in three Indianapolis 500s (1989, 1990, 1993) and finished a best of 11th place. What country was Theys from?

    (a) Belgium
    (b) Denmark
    (c) Finland
    (d) Netherlands

38. North Tonawanda, NY, was the hometown of the 1960 Rookie of the Year and fastest qualifier, who happened to be 2.5 mph faster than the pole winner, Eddie Sachs. Who was this driver?

    (a) Don Branson
    (b) Jim Hurtubise
    (c) Lloyd Ruby
    (d) Bud Tinglestad

39. Lone Star J. R. (Johnny Rutherford) was born where?

    (a) Arlington, TX
    (b) Fort Worth, TX
    (c) Coffeyville, KS
    (d) Denver, CO

40. In 1920, Ralph DePalma dominated the "500" again, but faltered late in the race and finished fifth. A famous "automobile" name won the race. Who?

    (a) Arthur Chevrolet
    (b) Gaston Chevrolet
    (c) Louis Chevrolet
    (d) William Chevrolet

41. Three-time winner Johnny Rutherford qualified for his last "500" in 1988. How many years following his final "500" did J. R. unsuccessfully attempt to qualify before deciding to retire?

    (a) two years
    (b) three years
    (c) four years
    (d) five years

42. Steve Krisiloff raced in 11 Indy 500s. Where was he originally from?

    (a) Omaha, NE
    (b) Parsippany, NJ
    (c) Speedway, IN
    (d) St. Louis, MO

43. In 1991, four members of the same family raced against each other in the "500." What was the family?

(a) the Andrettis—Mario, Michael, Jeff, and John
(b) the Unsers—Al, Al Jr., Johnny, and Robby

44. In 1980, a third Sneva brother attempted to make the "500" field, eventually crashing in practice and realizing Indy was not for him. What was his name?

(a) Al
(b) Jan
(c) Tim
(d) Wayne

45. What driver lost his ride with Penske for the 1975 season after severely injuring an arm in a dirt-car race in Syracuse, NY?

(a) Gary Bettenhausen
(b) Jimmy Caruthers
(c) Mark Donohue
(d) David Hobbs

46. On the day after the 1963 race, which driver called Parnelli Jones a "cheater" and as a result ended up on the floor at the Speedway Motel?

(a) Jim Clark
(b) A. J. Foyt
(c) Eddie Sachs
(d) Rodger Ward

47.　Which "500" winner died racing just 16 days after winning the "500" at the same track (Altoona, PA) in which former "500" winners Howdy Wilcox and Joe Boyer were fatally injured?

(a) Billy Arnold
(b) Fred Frame
(c) Ray Keech
(d) George Souders

48.　What was Lloyd Ruby's hometown?

(a) Arlington, TX
(b) Fort Worth, TX
(c) Houston, TX
(d) Wichita Falls, TX

49.　Spike Gelhausen raced in five "500s." What was his real first name?

(a) Anthony
(b) David
(c) Daniel
(d) James

50.　In 1996, a ten-time "500" veteran, after a ten-year absence, was a surprise starter in the "500." Who was it?

(a) Racin Gardner
(b) Howdy Holmes
(c) Danny Ongais
(d) Tom Sneva

51.   What was Parnelli Jones's real first name?

  (a) Ebb
  (b) Elmer
  (c) Parnell
  (d) Rufus

52.   This driver, like several in his time, began his career as a riding mechanic. He was a riding mechanic for 1915 winner Ralph DePalma, who also happened to be his uncle. Who was he?

  (a) Peter DePaolo
  (b) Harlan Fengler
  (c) Dario Resta
  (d) Count Louis Zborowski

53.   America's highly decorated World War I flying ace, Captain Eddie Rickenbacker, was a race driver prior to going into the military. His highest finish was tenth. In how many "500s" did he start?

  (a) one
  (b) two
  (c) three
  (d) four

54.   Ralph Hepburn was fatally injured preparing to qualify the powerful Novi in 1948. What was Hepburn's age when he passed away?

  (a) 22
  (b) 32
  (c) 42
  (d) 52

55. Match the driver with his hometown.

Mario Andretti	(a) Nazareth, PA
Gary Bettenhausen	(b) Pittsburgh, PA
Len Sutton	(c) Portland, OR
Chip Ganassi	(d) Tinley Park, IL
Roger McCluskey	(e) Tucson, AZ

56. In 1982, defending champion Bobby Unser returned as a driver coach, rather than a driver. Who did he coach?

(a) Geoff Brabham
(b) Chip Ganassi
(c) Josele Garza
(d) Al Unser Jr.

57. What "500" winner had sight in only one eye?

(a) Tommy Milton
(b) Bobby Rahal
(c) Troy Ruttman
(d) Jacques Villeneuve

58. In 1948, a 37 year-old rookie, nicknamed "The Cinderella Man," established a new pattern around the track that basically still is used today and is still referred to as the groove. Who was this individual?

(a) Johnnie Parsons
(b) Jim Rathmann
(c) Bill Vukovich
(d) Lee Wallard

59. The 1972 winner Mark Donohue graduated from what university with a degree in mechanical engineering?

   (a) Brown University
   (b) Columbia University
   (c) Denison University
   (d) University of Virginia

60. At six feet, three inches tall and 265 pounds, who was the tallest and heaviest winner of the "500"?

   (a) Sam Hanks
   (b) Jim Rathmann
   (c) Troy Ruttman
   (d) Bill Vukovich

61. Two Indianapolis 500 winners were riding mechanics before becoming drivers. Which of the following were riders before winning as drivers?

   (a) Peter DePaolo
   (b) Tommy Milton
   (c) Jimmy Murphy
   (d) Louis Schneider

62. Who was the first third-generation (grandson) driver to attempt to compete in the "500"?

   (a) Marco Andretti
   (b) A. J. Foyt IV
   (c) Teddy Pilette
   (d) Robby Unser

63. Before Jim Rathmann changed his identity so that he would comply with driver age requirements, what was his name?

(a) Herb Porter
(b) Dick Rathmann
(c) Ebb Rose
(d) Dempsey Wilson

64. In 1987, what driver crashed in practice and sustained a serious head injury, which opened up a position on the Penske team for eventual winner Al Unser Sr.?

(a) Jim Crawford
(b) Danny Ongais
(c) Johnny Rutherford
(d) Danny Sullivan

65. What was the first father-son combination to compete against each other in the "500"?

(a) Mario and Michael Andretti
(b) Jim and James McElreath
(c) Johnnie Parsons and Johnny Parsons Jr.
(d) Al and Al Unser Jr.

66. Gordon Johncock was from which town?

(a) Flint, MI
(b) Hastings, MI
(c) Holland, MI
(d) Lansing, MI

67.	Vern Schuppan raced in three "500s" with a best finish of third in 1981. What country was he from?

(a) Australia
(b) Bulgaria
(c) England
(d) France

68.	Which driver had the almost unbelievable record of finishes from 1959 to 1964 of first, second, third, first, fourth, second and then failed to qualify in 1965?

(a) Jimmy Clark
(b) A. J. Foyt
(c) Parnelli Jones
(d) Rodger Ward

69.	What driver was diagnosed with cancer after the 1974 race, underwent successful treatment, qualified tenth, and finished 14th in 1975?

(a) Jimmy Caruthers
(b) Sheldon Kinser
(c) Rick Muther
(d) Jan Opperman

70. In 1953, on probably the hottest race day in history, with temperatures in the low 90s and ten of the 23 cars that went beyond 100 laps using relief drivers, what driver stopped for a relief driver and then collapsed and died from overheating? His car, with Bob Scott as relief driver, finished 12th.

(a) Alberto Ascari
(b) Ralph Hepburn
(c) Chet Miller
(d) Carl Scarborough

71. The 1990 and 1997 winner Arie Luyendyk speaks three languages. Which does he not speak?

(a) Dutch
(b) English
(c) French
(d) German

72. The 1986 winner Bobby Rahal was a graduate of what college?

(a) Denison
(b) Ohio State
(c) Toledo
(d) Wooster

73. How old was Lyn St. James in 1992 when she made her first "500"?

    (a) 35
    (b) 40
    (c) 45
    (d) 50

74. What was 1985 "spin and win" Indy 500 winner Danny Sullivan doing before pursuing auto racing?

    (a) car salesman
    (b) construction worker
    (c) insurance salesman
    (d) taxicab driver

75. Who was the only driver in "500" history to drive in the race with a full beard?

    (a) Michael Andretti
    (b) Chet Fillip
    (c) Herm Johnson
    (d) Bobby Rahal

76. Which multiple winner of the "500" pulled a rookie mistake in his first race by failing to buckle his helmet for the start?

    (a) A. J. Foyt
    (b) Rick Mears
    (c) Al Unser Sr.
    (d) Bobby Unser

77. Sarah Fisher made her "500" debut in 2000. How old was she?

    (a) 19 years old
    (b) 22 years old
    (c) 25 years old
    (d) 28 years old

78. Which was the only family to have three brothers qualify for the same Indy 500?

    (a) Andretti
    (b) Foyt
    (c) Unser
    (d) Whittington

79. At six feet, six inches tall, who was the tallest driver to race in the "500" mile race since Joel Thorne in 1941?

    (a) Jerry Grant
    (b) Sheldon Kinser
    (c) Chris Kneifel
    (d) Troy Ruttman

80. What columnist practiced in 1981 and 1982 before making the race in 1983 and 1984? He was injured in a serious accident in the 1984 race and would never race at Indy again.

    (a) Patrick Bedard
    (b) Mike Chandler
    (c) Chris Economaki
    (d) Sam Posey

81. What diminutive driver competed in six "500s" between 1979 and 1988, starting as high as second and finishing a best of sixth place while taking the checkered flag in each race?

   (a) Tom Bigelow
   (b) Derek Daly
   (c) Teo Fabi
   (d) Howdy Holmes

82. Who was the fourth driver to win back-to-back 500-mile races at Indy?

   (a) Helio Castroneves
   (b) Al Unser Sr.
   (c) Mauri Rose
   (d) Bill Vukovich

83. Teo Fabi, the 1983 rookie pole sitter, was accomplished at what other sport prior to taking up auto racing?

   (a) motorcycle racing
   (b) mountain biking
   (c) snow skiing
   (d) water skiing

84. Which Unser has not qualified and raced in the Indy 500?

    (a) Al Unser Sr.
    (b) Al Unser Jr.
    (c) Al Unser III
    (d) Bobby Unser
    (e) Jerry Unser
    (f) Johnny Unser
    (g) Robby Unser

85. In 1993, reigning F-1 champion Nigel Mansell decided to move to IndyCar racing. Whose ride did he take over? This driver happened to move to F-1 for the 1993 season.

    (a) Michael Andretti
    (b) Derek Daly
    (c) Emerson Fittipaldi
    (d) Stefan Johansson

86. After competing in 35 Indy 500s, in what year did A. J. Foyt announce his retirement on Pole Day morning?

    (a) 1990
    (b) 1993
    (c) 1996
    (d) 1999

87. What college did 1927 winner George Souders attend?

    (a) Ball State
    (b) Indiana State
    (c) Indiana University
    (d) Purdue University

88. Danica Patrick's hometown is what?

    (a) Belleville, IL
    (b) Chicago, IL
    (c) Roscoe, IL
    (d) Springfield, IL

89. Who was the first driver in Indy 500 history to climb the fence in victory celebration?

    (a) Helio Castroneves
    (b) Gil de Ferran
    (c) Juan Pablo Montoya
    (d) Tony Stewart

90. What driver was largely responsible for getting a group of ethanol producers involved in Indy racing?

    (a) Paul Dana
    (b) Brian Herta
    (c) Ryan Hunter-Reay
    (d) Jeff Simmons

91. In the 1950s, what driver, who went on to win the race, actually tore down his engine after qualifying and reassembled it for the race himself after his chief mechanic was called away because of a family emergency?

    (a) Jimmy Bryan
    (b) Sam Hanks
    (c) Bob Sweikert
    (d) Bill Vukovich

92. Who was the first Englishman since Graham Hill in 1966 to win the "500"?

    (a) Kenny Brack
    (b) Eddie Cheever
    (c) Nigel Mansell
    (d) Dan Wheldon

93. How were 1919 winner Howdy Wilcox and 1932 second-place finisher Howdy Wilcox II related?

    (a) brothers
    (b) father and son
    (c) not related
    (d) uncle and nephew

94. In 1916, Ralph DePalma did not defend his title because of what?

    (a) injury
    (b) no appearance money offered
    (c) lack of funding
    (d) lack of nerve

95. Who has the highest finish in the "500" by a Japanese driver?

(a) Hideshi Matsuda
(b) Hiro Matsushita
(c) Hideki Mutoh
(d) Tora Takagi

96. Ray Harroun's nickname was what?

(a) the Bedouin
(b) the Magician
(c) the Mirror Man
(d) the Penguin

97. Pat O'Connor was from where?

(a) Mount Vernon, IL
(b) Mount Vernon, IN
(c) North Vernon, IN
(d) Scottsburg, IN

98. In 1923, race winner Tommy Milton was relieved by Howdy Wilcox between laps 103 and 151 because of what?

(a) blistered hands
(b) blurred vision
(c) cramping muscles
(d) motion sickness

99. Jigger Sirois's full given name was what?

(a) Fred Frame Sirois
(b) Leon Duray Sirois
(c) Thomas Milton Sirois
(d) Wilbur Shaw Sirois

100. Cliff Bergere, a 16-time "500" starter and one-time pole sitter, also was what?

(a) airplane mechanic
(b) Hollywood stuntman
(c) Las Vegas dealer
(d) taxicab driver

101. The real name of Leon Duray, the "Flying Frenchman," who was actually from Philadelphia, was what?

(a) George Stewart
(b) George Steward
(c) Steward George
(d) Steward Georgia

102. Graham Hill was a two-time Formula One world driving champion as well as the 1966 Indy 500 champion. How did he lose his life in 1975?

(a) airplane crash
(b) automobile crash
(c) boating accident
(d) racecar crash

103. Dick Simon raced in 17 Indianapolis 500s with a best finish of sixth. What did Simon do before going to IndyCar racing?

    (a) automobile dealership owner
    (b) dentist
    (c) insurance company executive
    (d) restaurant owner

104. In Dick Simon's last Indy 500 in 1988, how old was he?

    (a) 45
    (b) 50
    (c) 55
    (d) 60

105. Tom Sneva won the 1983 "500" and finished second three times, started from the pole three times, and was actually the fastest qualifier four times. How did Sneva make a living while he honed his racing skills?

    (a) airline pilot
    (b) automobile salesman
    (c) insurance salesman
    (d) assistant high school principal

106. The very personable Eddie Sachs drove in eight 500-mile races with a best finish of second in 1961. He won the pole position in 1960 and 1961. Besides his racing endeavors, what type of business did he own?

    (a) automobile repair shop
    (b) horse barns
    (c) taxi business
    (d) tavern

107. Who was called the Clown Prince of Auto Racing?

    (a) Tom Bigelow
    (b) Eddie Cheever
    (c) Jim Hurtubise
    (d) Eddie Sachs

108. Soon after winning the 1980 rookie of the year award, this driver started a successful NASCAR career which spanned through most of the 1980's. Who was this driver?

    (a) Bobby Allison
    (b) Donnie Allison
    (c) Paul Goldsmith
    (d) Tim Richmond

109. Between 1947 and 1950, Bill Holland scored finishes of second, second, first, and second. Holland owned what as a sideline business to his racing?

     (a) bowling alley
     (b) cab business
     (c) go-kart track
     (d) roller-skating rink

110. Two-time winner Bill Vukovich was sometimes called what?

     (a) Igor the Great
     (b) Mad Russian
     (c) Spooky Vuky
     (d) Wild Russian

111. What driver started in the second position in 1998, 1999, and 2001 and started on the pole in 2000?

     (a) Billy Boat
     (b) Kenny Brack
     (c) Arie Luyendyk
     (d) Greg Ray

112. In 1969, Al Unser, one of the pre-race favorites and fastest drivers in practice was injured in a motorcycle accident prior to qualifications. Who replaced him in the Vel's Parnelli Jones Lola for qualifications and the "500"?

(a) Arnie Knepper
(b) Mike Mosley
(c) Art Pollard
(d) Bud Tinglestad

113. Which of the following drivers received the Rookie of the Year award?

(a) Milka Duno
(b) Sarah Fisher
(c) Janet Guthrie
(d) Danica Patrick
(e) Lyn St. James

114. In 1966, who did Graham Hill replace on the Mecom Racing Team after this driver had been fatally injured practicing for the 24-Hours of Le Mans?

(a) Jim Clark
(b) Gary Congdon
(c) Walt Hansgen
(d) Jochen Rindt

115. Name the fan favorite who was able to lead the "500" in five of the six races between 1966 and 1971, but was unable to win?

    (a) Jim Hurtubise
    (b) Lloyd Ruby
    (c) George Snider
    (d) Jackie Stewart

116. What is the only number A. J. Foyt did not use at Indy during his career?

    (a) #1
    (b) #2
    (c) #5
    (d) #6
    (e) #7
    (f) #8
    (g) #9
    (h) #10
    (i) #14
    (j) #29

117. A. J. Foyt won the 1967 race for his third victory. His car that day was #14. After the 1967 win, he used several numbers other than #14. In what year did he start using #14 again, using it in every race thereafter?

    (a) 1970
    (b) 1973
    (c) 1977
    (d) 1982

118. Which popular driver was severely burned in an accident at Milwaukee in 1964 and had his fingers formed so that he could grip the steering wheel in order to race?

(a) Billy Foster
(b) Jim Hurtubise
(c) Gordon Johncock
(d) Mel Kenyon

119. Which driver drove relief in the race one year and then won the race the next year? He was considered a rookie winner, because he had not qualified the previous year and had not started the race.

(a) Ralph DePalma
(b) Louis Meyer
(c) Mauri Rose
(d) Wilbur Shaw

120. Which driver attempted unsuccessfully to make the race for six years before qualifying in his seventh year, winning the Rookie of the Year award?

(a) Bobby Grim
(b) Ralph Liguori
(c) Al Loquasto
(d) Bill Puterbaugh

121. Six-time Indianapolis 500 starter Howdy Holmes's family business produced what product?

    (a) cooking oil
    (b) Jiffy Mix
    (c) Jiffy Pop
    (d) Pop-Tarts

122. What was five-time "500" starter Shorty Templeman's real first name?

    (a) Anthony
    (b) Clark
    (c) Duane
    (d) George

123. What was Jim Hurtubise's favorite car number?

    (a) #56
    (b) #59
    (c) #91
    (d) #99

1911 winner Ray Harroun in the Marmon Wasp.

Chapter 2
Track/Facility

124. In what year did a 13 year-old boy named Tony Hulman see his first race?

    (a) 1914
    (b) 1924
    (c) 1934
    (d) 1946

125. What did the locals call the property on which the Indianapolis Motor Speedway was built?

    (a) The Old Allison Farm
    (b) The Old Fisher Farm
    (c) The Old Lilly Farm
    (d) The Old Pressley Farm

126. The angle of banking in each turn is?

    (a) nine degrees and 12 minutes
    (b) 12 degrees and nine minutes
    (c) 18 degrees and nine minutes
    (d) 24 degrees and 12 minutes

127. The current IMS Hall of Fame Museum was opened in time for what "500"?

    (a) 1971
    (b) 1976
    (c) 1981
    (d) 1986

128. In what year was the entire track repaved with asphalt for the first time?

    (a) 1956
    (b) 1966
    (c) 1976
    (d) 1986

129. Footage for the movie Winning, starring Paul Newman was shot in what year at IMS?

    (a) 1958
    (b) 1968
    (c) 1978
    (d) 1988

130. The pacer light system for caution periods was implemented in what year?

    (a) 1970
    (b) 1972
    (c) 1974
    (d) 1976

131. In what year was the original Speedway Museum opened?

    (a) 1946
    (b) 1951
    (c) 1956
    (d) 1961

132. How much was the original estimate for Speedway owners (Carl Fisher, James Allison, Arthur Newby, and Frank Wheeler) to purchase the property and build the Speedway?

    (a) $120,000
    (b) $220,000
    (c) $320,000
    (d) $420,000

133. For the 2002 "500" the SAFER barriers had been installed in each of the corners. Who spearheaded this innovative safety program?

    (a) A.J. Foyt
    (b) Chip Ganassi
    (c) Tony George
    (d) Roger Penske

134. By 1940, the so-called Brickyard track surface was actually only bricked on about 650 yards of the front stretch. For what race were those bricks covered, only leaving the Yard of Bricks at the start/finish line?

    (a) 1946
    (b) 1951
    (c) 1956
    (d) 1962

135. The second competitive race held at the Speedway occurred in August of 1909 and was which?

    (a) automobile race
    (b) balloon race
    (c) bicycle race
    (d) motorcycle race

136. In August of 1927, Eddie Rickenbacker and several colleagues purchased the Indianapolis Motor Speedway from Carl Fisher and James Allison for approximately how much?

    (a) $700,000
    (b) $1,000,000
    (c) $1,500,000
    (d) $2,000,000

137. In the autumn of 1909, the track surface was bricked, replacing the crushed rock and tar that had caused problems during the pre-"500" events. How many bricks were used?

    (a) 220,000
    (b) 2,200,000
    (c) 3,200,000
    (d) 5,200,000

138. After Joe Cloutier's death in December of 1989, Tony George was named president of the Indianapolis Motor Speedway at what age?

    (a) 25 years old
    (b) 30 years old
    (c) 35 years old
    (d) 40 years old

139. In what year did it rain heavily for several days, prompting the so-called Cagle Miracle? Clarence Cagle, the grounds superintendent, supervised the pumping of several hundred thousand gallons of rainwater from the tunnels beneath the track in order for the race to be held.

    (a) 1956
    (b) 1961
    (c) 1966
    (d) 1971

140. On race day of 1941, a garage fire caused havoc in Gasoline Alley. How many qualified cars were eliminated as a result of the fire?

    (a) zero
    (b) one
    (c) three
    (d) seven

141. In what year was the first race for the new ten-story pagoda structure at IMS?

    (a) 1990
    (b) 1995
    (c) 2000
    (d) 2005

142. In what year was the Japanese-style pagoda replaced by the Master Control Tower?

    (a) 1957
    (b) 1961
    (c) 1965
    (d) 1969

143. Match the part of the track with the distance of each.

    corners   (a) 1/8 mile
    short chutes   (b) 1/4 mile
    straights   (c) 5/8 mile

144. In what year were women generally allowed to enter the pits and garage area for the first time?

    (a) 1961
    (b) 1966
    (c) 1971
    (d) 1976

145. Who was the individual most responsible for the origination of the Indianapolis Motor Speedway and the Indianapolis 500?

    (a) James Allison
    (b) Carl Fisher
    (c) Anton Hulman Jr.
    (d) Eddie Rickenbacker

146. Tony Hulman purchased the Indianapolis Motor Speedway in 1945 for approximately how much?

    (a) $500,000
    (b) $700,000
    (c) $1,000,000
    (d) $1,500,000

147. In what year was the public-address system used on practice days for the first time?

    (a) 1947
    (b) 1957
    (c) 1967
    (d) 1977

148. Which "500" flagman preceded Pat Vidan?

    (a) Charlie Brockman
    (b) Frankie Del Roy
    (c) Shim Malone
    (d) Bill Vandewater

149. There was a gentleman from Indianapolis who worked as an investment broker; he was the intermediary between Wilbur Shaw and Mr. Anton Hulman Jr. He initiated the relationship between the two, resulting in Hulman's purchase of the track. Who was this intermediary?

(a) Joseph Cloutier
(b) Homer Cochran
(c) Pop Myers
(d) Joe Quinn

150. The first competitive event held at the Speedway occurred on June 5, 1909, and was what?

(a) automobile race
(b) balloon race
(c) bicycle race
(d) motorcycle race

151. In what year were the wooden garages replaced with the current concrete garages?

(a) 1955
(b) 1965
(c) 1975
(d) 1985

152. In what year was the original golf course opened? The course offered nine holes inside the track and nine holes east of the backstretch.

    (a) 1919
    (b) 1929
    (c) 1949
    (d) 1958

153. In what year were warning lights placed at six points around the track to signify either green or yellow track conditions?

    (a) 1935
    (b) 1940
    (c) 1945
    (d) 1950

154. Match the name of the president of IMS with the tenure as president:

    James Allison   (a) 1909–1923
    Joie Chitwood III   (b) 1923–1927
    Joe Cloutier, first tenure (c) 1927–1945
    Joe Cloutier, second tenure (d) 1945–1954
    John Cooper   (e) 1954–1977
    Carl Fisher   (f) 1977–1979
    Tony George   (g) 1979–1982
    Tony Hulman   (h) 1982–1989
    Eddie Rickenbacker   (i) 1989–2004
    Wilbur Shaw   (j) 2004–2009

155. The 500 Festival Parade was held in the evening during race week until which year, when it was changed to Saturday afternoon?

    (a) 1961
    (b) 1965
    (c) 1970
    (d) 1973

156. The original founder of the Speedway, Carl Fisher, was responsible for developing what?

    (a) Atlantic City
    (b) Hollywood
    (c) Miami Beach
    (d) Opryland

157. How long did it take to brick the track?

    (a) 63 days
    (b) 123 days
    (c) 223 days
    (d) 363 days

158. What airline did Eddie Rickenbacker take over, resulting in less personal involvement in the Speedway?

    (a) American Airlines
    (b) Eastern Airlines
    (c) Trans World Airlines
    (d) United Airlines

159. What radio announcer, who called the race from 1952 to 1976, first used this phrase before commercials: "Please stay tuned to the greatest spectacle in racing"?

    (a) Jerry Baker
    (b) Sid Collins
    (c) Mike Joy
    (d) Mike King

160. In what year did Pat Vidan begin his illustrious career as "500" flagman?

    (a) 1952
    (b) 1962
    (c) 1972
    (d) 1982

161. What year was the 500-mile race moved to Sunday, where it has remained ever since?

    (a) 1964
    (b) 1974
    (c) 1984
    (d) 1994

162. In what year did the 500 Festival Committee begin to choose a queen and a court from 33 princesses who were students from colleges located in the state of Indiana?

    (a) 1957
    (b) 1959
    (c) 1961
    (d) 1963

163. What year were rumble strips and a warm-up lane added to the track? The rumble strips were removed in 1996.

    (a) 1973
    (b) 1983
    (c) 1993
    (d) 1995

164. The racing film To Please a Lady, starring Clark Gable and Barbara Stanwyck, was filmed at the Speedway in what year?

    (a) 1930
    (b) 1940
    (c) 1950
    (d) 1960

165. Match the Indy 500 flagman with his tenure. One of the individuals had two stints.

    Brian Howard   (a) 1925–1927
    Seth Klein   (b) 1934–1953
    Seth Klein   (c) 1954–1961
    Duane Sweeney   (d) 1962–1979
    Bill Vandewater   (e) 1980–1996
    Pat Vidan   (f) 1997–present

166. What company sponsored the Rookie of the Year award in its initial year? The award was first presented in 1952, and this sponsor continued to support it through 1977.

   (a) American Fletcher National Bank
   (b) Pure Oil
   (c) Standard Oil
   (d) Stark and Wetzel

167. In what year was a second pre-race lap added (the parade lap)?

   (a) 1937
   (b) 1947
   (c) 1957
   (d) 1967

168. When Tony Hulman purchased the Indianapolis Motor Speedway in the fall of 1945, who did he appoint as president and general manager?

   (a) Joseph Cloutier
   (b) Pop Myers
   (c) Joe Quinn
   (d) Wilbur Shaw

169. Tony Hulman owned what successful company prior to purchasing the Indianapolis Motor Speedway in 1945?

   (a) Bowes Seal Fast
   (b) Clabber Girl Corporation
   (c) Kennedy Tank
   (d) Prest-O-Lite

170. In what year did the singing of "Back Home Again in Indiana" become a pre-race tradition?

    (a) 1911
    (b) 1930
    (c) 1946
    (d) 1961

171. Match the tenure with the Speedway's chief steward or director of racing.

Brian Barnhart	(a) 1919–1934
Tom Binford	(b) 1935–1939
Ted Doescher	(c) 1940–1941
Eddie Edenburn	(d) 1946–1948
Harlan Fengler	(e) 1949–1952
Harry McQuinn	(f) 1953–1957
Jack Mehan	(g) 1958–1973
Charlie Merz	(h) 1974–1995
Tommy Milton	(i) 1996–1997
Keith Ward	(j) 1998–present

172. What year did the American Society of Professional Automobile Racing (ASPAR) unsuccessfully threaten to have its drivers and cars boycott the "500"?

    (a) 1937
    (b) 1947
    (c) 1957
    (d) 1967

173. How wide are the main straightaways?

   (a) 30 feet
   (b) 40 feet
   (c) 50 feet
   (d) 60 feet

174. In what year was the formation of three-cars per row initiated for the start of the race? That grid line-up remains today.

   (a) 1911
   (b) 1921
   (c) 1931
   (d) 1941

175. Who were the four original founding fathers of the Indianapolis Motor Speedway?

   (a) James Allison
   (b) Carl Fisher
   (c) Anton Hulman Jr.
   (d) Pop Myers
   (e) Arthur Newby
   (f) Barnie Oldfield
   (g) Eddie Rickenbacker
   (h) Wilbur Shaw
   (i) Frank Wheeler

176. In what year was the pace car first presented to the winner of the race—a tradition that has continued every year since?

    (a) 1936
    (b) 1946
    (c) 1956
    (d) 1966

177. Wilbur Shaw, president of the Speedway, was killed in the fall of 1954. What caused his untimely death?

    (a) airplane crash
    (b) automobile crash
    (c) race-car crash
    (d) train crash

178. How wide is the track in the turns?

    (a) 40 feet
    (b) 60 feet
    (c) 80 feet
    (d) 100 feet

179. What was the last year in which the entire track surface was brick?

    (a) 1925
    (b) 1935
    (c) 1945
    (d) 1955

180. By what race were the inside walls taken down and safety aprons added? New outside walls were also built at a sharper angle, so that cars wouldn't launch.

   (a) 1936
   (b) 1946
   (c) 1956
   (d) 1966

181. In what year was the 500 Festival formed to coordinate a number of race-related celebrations?

   (a) 1946
   (b) 1947
   (c) 1957
   (d) 1962

182. What college did Tony Hulman attend while starring in athletics?

   (a) Harvard
   (b) Indiana State
   (c) Rose Hulman
   (d) Yale

1930 winner Billy Arnold with riding mechanic
and Hollywood stuntman Spider Matlock.

Chapter 3
Owners/Teams

183. What team of brothers actually drove their entered race car to the Speedway from Chicago for their first attempt at participating in the Indianapolis 500?

    (a) Arthur, Gaston, and Louis Chevrolet
    (b) Andy, Joe, and Vince Granatelli
    (c) Bill, Dale, and Don Whittington

184. What was the first year that Roger Penske competed at the "500" as a car owner?

    (a) 1968
    (b) 1969
    (c) 1970
    (d) 1971

185. Bobby Rahal's 1986 victory was a sweet tribute to his car owner, who succumbed to cancer just 11 days later. Who was the car owner?

    (a) Andy Granatelli
    (b) Jim Hall
    (c) Doug Shierson
    (d) Jim Trueman

186. Who was the first top CART team to come back to the Speedway for the 2000 race after the so-called IRL/CART split?

(a) Ganassi Racing
(b) Newman Haas Racing
(c) Penske Racing
(d) Rahal/Letterman Racing

187. What race team had the most cars in an Indy 500 (seven cars)?

(a) Menard Racing
(b) Penske Racing
(c) Sherman Armstrong Racing
(d) Team Scandia

188. In 1972, which driver was not part of Vel's Parnelli Jones Racing "Super Team"?

(a) Mario Andretti
(b) Joe Leonard
(c) Al Unser
(d) Bobby Unser

189. In 1977, Gary Bettenhausen drove for what flamboyant sponsor?

(a) Sherman Armstrong
(b) Ted Field
(c) James Garner
(d) Evil Knievel

190. In 1997, what racing team finished first and second—the first time such a coup had occurred since Leader Card did it in 1962 with Rodger Ward and Len Sutton?

    (a) A. J. Foyt Racing
    (b) Menard Racing
    (c) Penske Racing
    (d) Treadway Racing

191. Danny Ongais teamed with what department store-owning family member to lead the successful Interscope Special team in the late 1970s to mid-1980s?

    (a) Ted Field
    (b) John Menard
    (c) Richard Neiman
    (d) Stuart Sears

192. In 1965, Mario Andretti drove his rookie race for Al Dean in the Dean Van Lines Special. What multiple-winning driver also drove for Dean in his rookie year while finishing in 16th place?

    (a) A. J. Foyt
    (b) Johnny Rutherford
    (c) Al Unser Sr.
    (d) Bobby Unser

193. What popular band leader sponsored Sam Hanks in his third 500-mile race in 1946?

    (a) Desi Arnaz
    (b) Cab Calloway
    (c) Spike Jones
    (d) Lawrence Welk

194. Andy Granatelli's STP stood for what?

    (a) scientifically tested product
    (b) special transmission product
    (c) special treated petroleum
    (d) scientifically treated petroleum

195. Prior to Roger Penske, which car entrant had the most "500" victories?

    (a) J. C. Agajanian
    (b) Mike Boyle
    (c) Louis Meyer
    (d) Lou Moore

196. In 1948, this eventually famous car owner unsuccessfully attempted to qualify for the "500" as a driver. Who was it?

    (a) Andy Granatelli
    (b) Lindsey Hopkins
    (c) George Salih
    (d) Bob Wilke

197. To whom did Pat Patrick sell his racing team?

    (a) Chip Ganassi
    (b) Barry Green
    (c) Bobby Rahal
    (d) Sam Schmidt

198. In 1992, Scott Goodyear was bumped from the field, but a sponsor's contractual stipulation required him to replace the driver of his qualified backup car and compete in the race. Goodyear went on to start 33rd and finish 0.043 seconds behind the winner. Who did he replace?

    (a) Eric Bachelart
    (b) Brian Bonner
    (c) Mike Groff
    (d) Ted Prappas

199. In 1965, who was the teammate for the winner, Jim Clark?

    (a) Dan Gurney
    (b) Bobby Johns
    (c) Arnie Knepper
    (d) Mickey Rupp

200. For the 1967 "500," two Mallard-Offenhausers were entered. Jim Hurtubise was assigned to one car. Who drove the other?

    (a) Chuck Hulse
    (b) Ebb Rose
    (c) Bob Veith
    (d) Carl Williams

201. Mark Donohue retired at the end of 1973. Peter Revson was to replace Donohue at Penske Racing for the 1974 race, but was fatally injured testing for the South African Grand Prix in March of 1974. Who replaced Revson on the Penske team?

(a) Mike Hiss
(b) David Hobbs
(c) Mike Mosley
(d) Tom Sneva

202. What sponsor poured 150 silver dollars into Parnelli Jones's helmet when he became the first driver to officially eclipse 150 mph, and 200 silver dollars into Tom Sneva's helmet when he officially eclipsed 200 mph?

(a) J. C. Agajanian
(b) Phil Hedback
(c) Pat Patrick
(d) Roger Penske

203. In 1988, what team's three cars occupied the entire front row? This was the only time one team had accomplished this.

(a) Foyt Racing
(b) Newman/Haas Racing
(c) Patrick Racing
(d) Penske Racing

204. What chief mechanic recorded seven victories with A. J. Foyt, Graham Hill, Al Unser Sr., Gordon Johncock, and Tom Sneva?

    (a) George Bignotti
    (b) Clint Brawner
    (c) Jim McGee
    (d) A. J. Watson

205. In the mid-1990s, Scandia Racing began competing in the "500." Scandia was formerly what racing team?

    (a) Bettenhausen Motorsports
    (b) Galles Racing
    (c) Kelley Racing
    (d) Simon Racing

206. Who were the first drivers to score a one-two finish in the "500" for Roger Penske?

    (a) Castroneves/de Ferran
    (b) Donohue/Bettenhausen
    (c) Mears/Unser Jr.
    (d) Mears/Unser Sr.

207. In the 1920s (1920–1929) which car builder's cars won five times, took second place twice, and took third place twice?

    (a) Louis Chevrolet
    (b) Cliff Durant
    (c) Fred Duesenberg
    (d) Harry Miller

208. The Nordyke and Marmon Automobile Company won the first 500-mile race with Ray Harroun as the driver in 1911. In 1912, Joe Dawson won the race in a National. What did each of these automobile companies decide to do after winning the "500"?

(a) wrest on their laurels and cease their racing program
(b) change the Marmon Wasp from #32 to #1 and change the National from #8 to #1
(c) expand their racing program
(d) switch to a rear-engine car

209. In 1969, Andy Granatelli, desperate to win Indy on his 17th try, entered how many cars?

(a) three
(b) five
(c) seven
(d) 11

210. In 1955, for whom was Bill Vukovich driving when he was fatally injured in a multi-car crash while leading and attempting to win his third consecutive "500"?

(a) J. C. Agajanian
(b) Al Dean
(c) Lindsey Hopkins
(d) Howard Keck

211. The last year that Team Lotus participated in the month of May was in 1969. What foreign team would arrive the next year and almost immediately begin to make a strong impact?

    (a) Chaparral
    (b) Lola
    (c) McLaren
    (d) Mercedes

1939 and 1940 winner Wilbur Shaw in the Boyle Maserati.

Chapter 4
Race Information

212. On lap 105 of the 2008 race, Tony Kanaan was eliminated in an accident that he blamed on one of his teammates. Who was it?

   (a) Marco Andretti
   (b) Hideki Mutoh
   (c) Danica Patrick

213. After the death of Tony Hulman in the autumn of 1977, who voiced the command of "Lady and gentlemen, start your engines" in May of 1978?

   (a) Joseph Cloutier
   (b) Mary Fendrich Hulman
   (c) Mari Hulman George
   (d) Tony George

214. Who was the 500 Festival Queen in 1961 for the 50th Anniversary Golden 500?

   (a) Candy Cluster
   (b) Suzanne Devine
   (c) Diane Hunt
   (d) Mimi Littlejohn

215. Which Indianapolis 500 winner survived all of the following and still won the race?

- A pit-stop blunder that resulted in a stop-and-go penalty in the last 50 laps
- Trailing the leader by more than 30 seconds with 30 laps left.
- A last-lap pass for the lead—the only one in the history of the "500."

(a) Helio Castroneves
(b) Sam Hornish Jr.
(c) Gordon Johncock
(d) Rick Mears

216. In 1995, winner Jacques Villeneuve overcame what in winning the race?

(a) broken wing
(b) one-lap penalty for passing the pace car
(c) one-lap penalty for leaking fluid
(d) two-lap penalty for passing the pace car

217. In 1992, Michael Andretti dominated the race leading 160 laps. The infamous Andretti Jinx then struck after completing how many laps?

(a) 179
(b) 184
(c) 189
(d) 194

218. In 2002, it appeared that a rookie might win the race for the third consecutive year until what driver went high in turn four while leading and hit the wall on lap 173?

    (a) Alex Barron
    (b) Tony Kanaan
    (c) Max Papis
    (d) Tomas Scheckter

219. Match the driver with the year of the top finishes of the Kennedy Tank Special, which competed in the "500" seven times.

Les Anderson	(a) eighth, 1936
George Barringer	(b) 11th, 1947
Bill Cantrell	(c) 15th, 1940
Joie Chitwood	(d) 21st, 1949

220. Who was leading the race in 1981 when a major pit fire took him out on lap 58?

    (a) Mario Andretti
    (b) Josele Garza
    (c) Rick Mears
    (d) Tom Sneva

221. In 1992, the pole sitter crashed on the parade lap as a result of cold temperatures and tires. Who was it?

    (a) Scott Goodyear
    (b) Roberto Guerrero
    (c) Scott Sharp
    (d) Tom Sneva

222. Al Unser in his Johnny Lightning Special dominated the "500" in 1970 to the extent of leading how many laps?

(a) 181
(b) 186
(c) 190
(d) 196

223. In 1970, who lost control of his car just prior to the start due to a half-shaft failure? This failure resulted in a brief red-flag situation before the race even started.

(a) George Follmer
(b) Jim Malloy
(c) Art Pollard
(d) Greg Weld

224. In 1966, Jim Clark, the "500" defending champion, spun how many times during the race? This resulted in a second-place finish, rather than a victory.

(a) one time
(b) two times
(c) three times
(d) four times

225. Match the shortened "500" with the number of laps completed.

1926 (a)   102 laps
1950 (b)   133 laps
1973 (c)   138 laps
1975 (d)   160 laps
1976 (e)   166 laps
2004 (f)   174 laps
2007 (g)   180 laps

226. The last pure relief driver was used in 1977 by John Mahler. Who relieved him?

(a) Larry "Boom Boom" Cannon
(b) Steve Krisiloff
(c) Jan Opperman
(d) Bill Puterbaugh

227. In 1947, the EZY sign cost what driver a first-place finish?

(a) Fred Agabashian
(b) Melvin "Tony" Bettenhausen
(c) Bill Holland
(d) Ted Horn

228. In 1926, rookie Frank Lockhart won a rain-shortened "500" by two laps over second place. How many actual miles did Lockhart complete?

(a) 300 miles
(b) 350 miles
(c) 400 miles
(d) 450 miles

229. Match the driver with his hometown.

Spike Gelhausen	(a) Bloomington, IN
Parnelli Jones	(b) Jasper, IN
Pete Halsmer	(c) Lafayette, IN
Mel Kenyon	(d) Lebanon, IN
Sheldon Kinser	(e) Torrance, CA

230. Match the anchor for the radio broadcast with his tenure in the job:

Sid Collins	(a)	1952–1976
Bob Jenkins	(b)	1977–1987
Mike King	(c)	1988–1989
Paul Page	(d)	1990–1998
Lou Palmer	(e)	1999–present

231. In the 1975 "500," this veteran drove car #40 Wildcat for Patrick Racing. He led from lap 97 to 161, with the exception of pit stops, before a mechanical problem ended his day. Who was this driver?

(a) Wally Dallenbach
(b) Steve Krisiloff
(c) Graham McRae
(d) Salt Walther

232. In the first "500," 40 cars started the race. How many cars were in each row for the so-called flying start, with the exception of the first and last row?

    (a) two
    (b) three
    (c) four
    (d) five

233. The 1924 race was unique in that co-winners were declared. Lora Corum drove the first 111 laps and was in fourth position when he was replaced by whom (who went on to win the race)?

    (a) Joe Boyer
    (b) Peter DePaolo
    (c) Frank Lockhart
    (d) George Souders

234. In 1965, which NASCAR team was brought in to handle Jim Clark's pit stops?

    (a) Allison Brothers
    (b) Marlin Brothers
    (c) Team Petty
    (d) Wood Brothers

235. What was the first year in which there were no front-engine cars in the "500"?

    (a) 1965
    (b) 1967
    (c) 1969
    (d) 1971

236. In 1971, with less than 100 miles to go, Mike Mosley crashed in turn four and collected Bobby Unser before colliding with the retired parked car of Mark Donohue. What driver stopped his car and helped Mosley from his burning car?

(a) Mario Andretti
(b) Gary Bettenhausen
(c) Billy Vukovich
(d) Denny Zimmerman

237. In 1953, Bill Vukovich dominated the race with temperatures on race day of over 90 degrees. How many laps did he lead?

(a) 165 laps
(b) 175 laps
(c) 185 laps
(d) 195 laps

238. In 1982, as the cars approached the start line, there was an accident. Which of the listed drivers was not involved?

(a) Mario Andretti
(b) A. J. Foyt
(c) Hector Rebaque
(d) Dale Whittington

239. In 2008, Danica Patrick was eliminated from the race in a pit collision on lap 171. What other driver was involved and eliminated in the same incident?

(a) Ryan Briscoe
(b) Helio Castroneves
(c) Tony Kanaan
(d) Tomas Scheckter

240. What winner won the race with a broken shock absorber and no brakes?

(a) A. J. Foyt, 1961
(b) Sam Hanks, 1957
(c) Parnelli Jones, 1963
(d) Lee Wallard, 1951

241. In 1998, with just over 60 laps to go, there were just three drivers on the lead lap. Which of the following drivers was not on the lead lap?

(a) Eddie Cheever Jr.
(b) Davey Hamilton
(c) Steve Knapp
(d) Buddy Lazier

242. What former winner and his riding mechanic traded injuries as a result of accidents in both the 1931 and 1932 races: broken shoulder (driver) and broken pelvis (riding mechanic) in 1931 and then broken pelvis (driver) and broken shoulder (riding mechanic) in 1932? The 1932 race would be the driver's final race, after which he moved to the West Coast and worked as a contractor.

(a) Billy Arnold
(b) Peter DePaolo
(c) Louis Meyer
(d) Louis Schneider

243. In 1994, Emerson Fittipaldi led a total of 145 laps before crashing on what lap while attempting to lap second-place Al Unser Jr.?

(a) 170
(b) 175
(c) 180
(d) 185

244. In 1986, what driver crashed on the pace lap as a result of a broken CV joint?

(a) Kevin Cogan
(b) Roberto Guerrero
(c) Tom Sneva
(d) Al Unser

245. The 1975 race, won by Bobby Unser, was shortened by rain on what lap?

(a) 170
(b) 174
(c) 178
(d) 182

246. In 2006, Michael Andretti came out of retirement and came very close to winning his first "500." How late in the race was Michael leading?

(a) lap 189
(b) lap 192
(c) lap 195
(d) lap 197

247. In 1988, Team Penske dominated. The three Penske drivers (Mears, Sullivan, and Unser Sr.) started in the front row and led how many of the 200 laps?

(a) 162 laps
(b) 172 laps
(c) 182 laps
(d) 192 laps

248. In 1965, Jim Clark led how many laps on his way to victory?

(a) 160
(b) 170
(c) 180
(d) 190

249. Match the winning driver and year with the number of laps led that year.

Billy Arnold, 1930   (a)   190
Jim Clark, 1965   (b)   190
Al Unser, 1970   (c)   195
Bill Vukovich, 1953 (d)   198

250. 1993 winner Emerson Fittipaldi elected to drink what in Victory Lane before the traditional milk?

(a) champagne
(b) Coca-Cola
(c) lemonade
(d) orange juice

251. In 1911, the estimated attendance at the inaugural race was

(a) 25,000
(b) 50,000
(c) 80,000
(d) 150,000

252. In what year were the final 100 miles run under yellow due to rain?

(a) 1926
(b) 1940
(c) 1975
(d) 1976

253. In what year was the Citizens of Indianapolis Lap Prize Fund initiated, paying $100 to the leader of each lap?

(a) 1911
(b) 1920
(c) 1940
(d) 1957

254. Tom Sneva won the 1983 race after finishing in second place how many times?

(a) one
(b) two
(c) three
(d) four

255. The 1937 finish became the closest in history (2.16 seconds) and held up as the closest for the next 45 years. Who nearly made up almost two minutes in the last 20 laps to eventually come just shy of overtaking Wilbur Shaw?

(a) Cliff Bergere
(b) Ralph Hepburn
(c) Ted Horn
(d) Louis Meyer

256. In the 2004 race, a rain delay caused a schedule conflict for Robby Gordon, who was attempting to compete in both the Indy 500 and the Charlotte 600 in the same day. Who substituted for Gordon so he could make the Charlotte race?

(a) Larry Foyt
(b) Richie Hearn
(c) Jaques Lazier
(d) Robby McGehee

257. Jim Nabors began singing "Back Home Again in Indiana" in 1972. In what state was Nabors born?

(a) Alabama
(b) California
(c) Indiana
(d) South Carolina

258. In what year was the Borg-Warner trophy unveiled?

(a) 1926
(b) 1936
(c) 1946
(d) 1956

259. Bobby Unser took the checkered flag as the winner in 1981. Who was declared the official winner the next morning and introduced as such at the Victory Banquet? One hundred and thirty-eight days later, Bobby Unser was reinstated as winner by an arbitration committee for USAC.

(a) Bill Alsup
(b) Mario Andretti
(c) Gordon Johncock
(d) Tom Sneva

260. In what year did Tom Carnegie begin his career on the public-address system at the Speedway?

(a) 1946
(b) 1951
(c) 1956
(d) 1961

261. In 1966, a spectacular crash just as the field was receiving the green flag, starting the race, eliminated how many cars?

(a) six
(b) nine
(c) 11
(d) 14

262. What was the only year in the history of the "500" in which there was a lead change on the last lap?

    (a) 1937
    (b) 1992
    (c) 2002
    (d) 2006

263. In 1960, there were more lead changes than in any other race. The last 14 were between winner Jim Rathmann and second-place finisher Rodger Ward alone. How many total lead changes took place?

    (a) 21
    (b) 25
    (c) 29
    (d) 33

264. The year 1986 resulted in the closest first, second, and third (1.881 seconds) finish in history. What driver was not part of this close finish?

    (a) Kevin Cogan
    (b) Roberto Guerrero
    (c) Rick Mears
    (d) Bobby Rahal

265. What driver had won consecutive "500s" when, in his attempt to win three straight, his wheel collapsed on lap 152 while leading, causing him to crash.

    (a) Louis Meyer
    (b) Mauri Rose
    (c) Wilbur Shaw
    (d) Bill Vukovich

266. In 1967, the Parnelli Jones turbine car dropped out while leading on what lap due to a broken transmission resulting from a $6 ball-bearing failure after having led a total of 171 laps?

    (a) 177
    (b) 187
    (c) 193
    (d) 197

267. In 1961, it appeared that Eddie Sachs was on his way to victory when late in the race he pitted for a right rear-tire replacement, relinquishing the lead to A. J. Foyt, who went on to win his first "500." On what lap did this occur?

    (a) lap 182
    (b) lap 187
    (c) lap 192
    (d) lap 197

268. In 1936, Louis Meyer celebrated in Victory Lane and started a tradition that has continued every race since with the exception of years 1947 to 1955 ("Water from Wilbur" years). He refreshed himself that day in Victory Lane with what?

(a) champagne
(b) Coca-Cola
(c) lemonade
(d) milk

269. In 1939, three-time winner Louis Meyer led from lap 135 until spinning in turn one on lap 182. Meyer lost the lead to Shaw and was trying to catch him when he uncharacteristically spun again and hit the inside fence on lap 198. By the time he climbed into the ambulance, he had made what decision?

(a) to change teams for next year
(b) to drive a rear engine car next year
(c) to drive a Maserati next year
(d) to retire from racing

270. What legendary racing family had the dubious distinction of finishing 32nd and 33rd in the 2004 race?

(a) Andretti
(b) Foyt
(c) Jones
(d) Unser

271. 1996 winner Buddy Lazier competed in the race, battling the effects of a serious injury that had occurred in April of that year. What was the injury?

(a) back fractures
(b) broken leg
(c) broken wrist
(d) severe concussion

272. In 1955, while leading, Bill Vukovich was collected in an accident when he tried to overtake a pack of cars which were two and three laps down. With whose car did Vukovich make contact before his car was launched over the backstretch retainer, fatally injuring the great two-time champion?

(a) Johnny Boyd
(b) Ed Elisian
(c) Al Keller
(d) Rodger Ward

273. In 1966, Englishman Graham Hill won the "500" as a rookie, becoming the first to win since George Souders* in 1927—but Hill did not win the Rookie of the Year award. Who dropped out while leading on lap 192 but won that prize?

(a) Mario Andretti
(b) Mel Kenyon
(c) Jackie Stewart
(d) Cale Yarborough

274. Since its inception in 1911, the Indianapolis 500 has been run every year, with the exception of how many years due to war involvement?

    (a) three years
    (b) six years
    (c) eight years
    (d) ten years

275. Due to rain returning after the race had been stopped previously, and about ready to restart, what winner walked to Victory Lane?

    (a) Gordon Johncock
    (b) Johnnie Parsons
    (c) Johnny Rutherford
    (d) Bobby Unser

276. Prior to Emerson Fittipaldi in 1993, what winner in the early 1980s refused to drink milk in Victory Lane?

    (a) Gordon Johncock
    (b) Johnny Rutherford
    (c) Tom Sneva
    (d) Bobby Unser

277. In 1952, Bill Vukovich appeared to be on his way to winning his first "500," leading by 22 seconds on lap 191 when the steering arm broke, ending his race. Who went on to win?

(a) Bill Holland
(b) Johnnie Parsons
(c) Troy Ruttman
(d) Lee Wallard

278. In 1999, Kenny Brack took the checkered flag first when who was forced to pit for fuel while leading with just over a lap to go?

(a) Billy Boat
(b) Robby Gordon
(c) Roberto Guerrero
(d) Eliseo Salazar

279. The 1911 race paid how much to the winner?

(a) $1,250
(b) $5,250
(c) $14,250
(d) $25,250

280. What NASCAR star raced at Indy in 1973 and 1975 for the Penske Team?

(a) Bobby Allison
(b) Donnie Allison
(c) Bobby Johns
(d) Lee Roy Yarbrough

281. In 1982, Gordon Johncock held off Rick Mears for his second "500" victory by how much?

    (a) 0.16 seconds
    (b) 0.56 seconds
    (c) 1.4 seconds
    (d) 7.8 seconds

282. Who hitched a ride back to the pit area with 1980 winner Johnny Rutherford on his victory lap?

    (a) Tony George
    (b) Jim Hall
    (c) Roger Rager
    (d) Tim Richmond

283. In what year did local TV station WFBM Channel 6 broadcast the race live?

    (a) 1949
    (b) 1959
    (c) 1969
    (d) 1979

284. It was reported the 1913 winner, Frenchman Jules Goux, refreshed himself during the race by drinking what on some of his pit stops?

    (a) champagne
    (b) lemonade
    (c) milk
    (d) orange juice

285. What Indy champion, in 29 "500s," started on the front row eight times and finished 30th or worse eight times?

(a) Mario Andretti
(b) A.J. Foyt
(c) Al Unser Sr.
(d) Bobby Unser

286. In what year did ABC switch from same-day delayed coverage to live coverage?

(a) 1966
(b) 1976
(c) 1986
(d) 1996

287. Which of these great drivers was not a four-time winner?

(a) A. J. Foyt
(b) Rick Mears
(c) Louis Meyer
(d) Al Unser Sr.

288. Floyd Roberts won the 1938 race. How many pit stops did he make?

(a) zero
(b) one
(c) two
(d) three

289. Joe Dawson won the second "500" in 1912. Ralph DePalma dominated nearly the entire race, leading by five and a half laps when he dropped out on lap 198. How many laps did DePalma lead?

(a) 98
(b) 150
(c) 176
(d) 196

290. In 1989, Danny Sullivan drove in the race with a

(a) broken ankle
(b) broken arm
(c) broken wrist
(d) sprained ankle

291. Who did Helio Castroneves hold off by literally inches to win the 2002 race when a yellow occurred on lap 199 just as this driver was attempting to pass Castroneves in turn three?

(a) Michael Andretti
(b) Gil de Ferran
(c) Tony Kanaan
(d) Paul Tracy

292. In 2005, rookie Danica Patrick led as late as what lap before being overtaken by Dan Wheldon?

(a) 190
(b) 193
(c) 196
(d) 199

293. The 1973 race was shortened by rain, and the red and checkered flags were waved together on the third race day after how many laps?

    (a) 133 laps
    (b) 143 laps
    (c) 153 laps
    (d) 163 laps

294. What was the year in which brightly colored balloons were released just prior to the race for the first time, giving birth to another tradition?

    (a) 1928
    (b) 1938
    (c) 1948
    (d) 1958

295. In 1941, car owner Lou Moore decided to replace current driver Floyd Davis, who was on lap 72 in 11th position and about two and a half minutes behind the leader Cliff Bergere. The replacement went on to win the race. Who was he?

    (a) Joe Boyer
    (b) Floyd Roberts
    (c) Mauri Rose
    (d) Wilbur Shaw

296. With less than 40 laps to go in the 2008 race, this perennial bridesmaid made a highlight pass to go from third to first on a zigzag, inside-outside pass. Who was it?

(a) Marco Andretti
(b) Scott Dixon
(c) Vitor Meira
(d) Dan Wheldon

297. In 1958, a month long speed duel between Dick Rathmann and what driver culminated in a horrendous crash involving 15 cars on the first lap in turn three when that driver spun and was hit by Rathmann?

(a) Ed Elisian
(b) Pat O'Connor
(c) Jerry Unser
(d) Bob Veith

298. In 1994, reigning national champion Nigel Mansell was running in third position on lap 92, under caution, when a bizarre accident occurred resulting in whose car landing on top of his car?

(a) Marco Greco
(b) Hideshi Matsuda
(c) John Paul Jr.
(d) Dennis Vitolo

299. What two defending "500" champions were fatally injured during the race the year after their wins?

(a) Bill Cummings
(b) Pat Flaherty
(c) Floyd Roberts
(d) Bill Vukovich

300. What winner received the checkered flag and just moments later had his throttle linkage break?

(a) Jimmy Bryan
(b) Pat Flaherty
(c) A. J. Foyt
(d) Graham Hill

301. In 1987, Mario Andretti dominated the race until slowing down on lap 177 with a one-lap lead on second-place Roberto Guerrero and a two-lap lead on third-place Al Unser Sr. How many laps did Mario lead?

(a) 150 laps
(b) 160 laps
(c) 170 laps
(d) 180 laps

302. In 1975, future winner Tom Sneva had a horrendous crash in turn two after hitting wheels with whom?

(a) Bobby Allison
(b) Mario Andretti
(c) Pancho Carter
(d) Eldon Rasmussen

303. In 1989, with just over one lap to go, Fittipaldi and Unser Jr. made contact. How many laps were they ahead of third-place runner Raul Boesel?

(a) one lap
(b) three laps
(c) five laps
(d) six laps

304. Who relieved Ray Harroun for about 100 miles in the first "500"?

(a) Joe Dawson
(b) Don Herr
(c) Ralph Mulford
(d) Cyrus Patchke

305. In 1997, rain on Sunday and Monday forced the race to be run on Monday and Tuesday. Prior to the first green flag, several incidents kept how many cars from taking the green flag?

(a) two cars
(b) three cars
(c) four cars
(d) five cars

306. Joie Chitwood III was named president of IMS in 2004. His grandfather was a seven-time starter in the "500," finishing fifth three times. In what year did he drive the Kennedy Tank Special to a 15th place finish?

    (a) 1930
    (b) 1940
    (c) 1950
    (d) 1960

307. In 1986, rain on Sunday and Monday postponed the race until when?

    (a) Tuesday
    (b) Wednesday
    (c) Saturday
    (d) Sunday

308. In 1997, a first occurred when three different drivers led the race in the last ten laps. Which driver was not one of the three?

    (a) Scott Goodyear
    (b) Buddy Lazier
    (c) Arie Luyendyk
    (d) Jeff Ward

309. What place did Danica Patrick finish in 2005 in her rookie "500"?

    (a) second
    (b) third
    (c) fourth
    (d) fifth

310. In 1927, a very memorable event occurred when a car came down the front straight on fire, looking like a blowtorch. While standing in the cockpit, the driver steered the car past the fuel-laden pits to avoid a possible fuel explosion and jumped from the car after passing the pits. Who was this courageous driver?

(a) Norm Batten
(b) Cliff Bergere
(c) Harry Hartz
(d) Ralph Hepburn

311. Race day 2004 was a battle with the weather. The race was stopped for a short time on lap 27 and finally called, (with Buddy Rice declared the winner) on what lap?

(a) 150
(b) 160
(c) 170
(d) 180

312. In 1926 and 1927, something occurred that did not occur again for almost 75 years. What was it?

(a) A new miles-per-hour average was set in successive years.
(b) The race was shortened due to rain in successive years.
(c) Rookies won the race in successive years.
(d) The winner was leading by more than one lap at the finish in successive years.

313. In 1977, Gordon Johncock dropped out while leading on what lap after having led for 85 of the previous 87 laps?

    (a) 182
    (b) 184
    (c) 186
    (d) 188

314. In the 1998 race, Eddie Cheever became the first owner/driver since A. J. Foyt in 1977 to win the race. Cheever was nearly collected in the first turn on the first lap by whom? He was able to avoid it and go on to win.

    (a) Donnie Beechler
    (b) Jack Miller
    (c) Billy Roe
    (d) J. J. Yeley

315. On lap 52 of the 1967 race, Parnelli Jones, (in the STP turbine) spun with another spinning driver, but both were able to continue. Who was the driver of the other car?

    (a) Jim Clark
    (b) Graham Hill
    (c) Cale Yarborough
    (d) Lee Roy Yarbrough

316. In 1968, eventual winner Bobby Unser had to overcome a significant mechanical problem during the race. What was it?

    (a) broken shock
    (b) burned piston
    (c) gearbox
    (d) lost wheel

317. In 1968, Joe Leonard, driving an STP turbine, dropped out while leading on lap 191. His teammate dropped out at virtually the same moment. Who was that teammate?

    (a) Graham Hill
    (b) Parnelli Jones
    (c) Art Pollard
    (d) Greg Weld

318. In 1971, Mark Donohue dominated the early stage of the race and then dropped out while leading on lap 66. At that point he had led 52 laps. In 1972, how many laps did Donohue lead while winning the "500"?

    (a) 13
    (b) 23
    (c) 53
    (d) 83

319. In 1973, on what day of the week were the red and checkered flags finally waved for the winner, Gordon Johncock?

    (a) Sunday
    (b) Monday
    (c) Tuesday
    (d) Wednesday

320. In 1986, Kevin Cogan passed both Rick Mears and Bobby Rahal for the lead on lap 188. A yellow on lap 195, after Cogan had pulled away, resulted in a bunch-up and an eventual pass on lap 198 by Rahal, who went on to victory. Who caused the late yellow?

    (a) Raul Boesel
    (b) Randy Lanier
    (c) Arie Luyendyk
    (d) Jacques Villeneuve

321. Which "500" winner ran the race's fastest lap on his 200th lap? This has occurred only once in "500" history.

    (a) Sam Hornish Jr.
    (b) Gordon Johncock
    (c) Bobby Rahal
    (d) Bill Vukovich

322. In the 1986 race, one of the all-time greats entered the pits too hot, spun, and made contact with the pit wall, ending his race. Who was it?

(a) Mario Andretti
(b) A. J. Foyt
(c) Johnny Rutherford
(d) Al Unser Sr.

323. In the 1987 race, Tony Bettenhausen lost a wheel, which was struck by another car. The contact with the loose wheel eventually caused a master cylinder leak, which cost this driver a victory. Who was this driver?

(a) Fabrizio Barbazza
(b) Gary Bettenhausen
(c) Roberto Guerrero
(d) Al Unser Jr.

324. In 1990, Emerson Fittipaldi led a total of 128 laps—by far the most by any driver that year. He might have won consecutive "500s," had it not been for what circumstance?

(a) bent wing
(b) blistered hands
(c) blistered tires
(d) running out of fuel

325. In 1992, after Roberto Guerrero hit the wall on the parade lap, who brought the field to the start and then, moments later, became sandwiched by Michael and Mario Andretti, dropping him to third place by the first turn?

(a) Eddie Cheever
(b) Bobby Rahal
(c) Tom Sneva
(d) Jimmy Vasser

326. In 1986, on Carb Day, Dennis Firestone severely crashed his qualified car. Unable to repair the car and lacking a backup, Firestone was forced to withdraw. Who was the first alternate to start the race as a result?

(a) Phil Krueger
(b) Ed Pimm
(c) Dick Simon
(d) Rich Vogler

327. The final pit stop by Team Penske for Rick Mears in the 1982 "500" may well have cost Mears the race, the stop taking five seconds longer than that by Gordon Johncock's Patrick Racing Team crew. Mears lost the race to Johncock by 0.16 seconds. What did the Penske crew do that used up the extra time?

(a) added more fuel than necessary to finish
(b) provided incorrect information to driver
(c) mounted wheel wrong
(d) adjusted wing incorrectly

328. On what lap did Tom Sneva pass both Al Unser Jr. and leader Al Unser Sr., going on to win the 1983 race after being blocked by Unser Jr. for several laps?

   (a) 161
   (b) 171
   (c) 181
   (d) 191

329. In 1966, what driver was involved in the main-stretch accident on lap one that eliminated 11 cars, but was able to repair his car and continue? He eventually finished fourth, but his actual time on the track was less than that of the winner, Graham Hill.

   (a) Sonny Ates
   (b) Don Branson
   (c) Billy Foster
   (d) Gordon Johncock

330. What was the first year in which A. J. Foyt led the first lap of the race?

   (a) 1961
   (b) 1964
   (c) 1977
   (d) 1982

331. In 1996, who did winner Buddy Lazier pass for the lead on lap 193?

(a) Roberto Guerrero
(b) Davy Jones
(c) Eliseo Salazar
(d) Alessandro Zampedri

332. In 1995, Scott Goodyear passed the pace car, coming to a restart while leading (and was subsequently penalized) on what lap? This very well could have cost him a win; he eventually finished 14th.

(a) 181
(b) 186
(c) 191
(d) 196

333. What driver in the 2000s won the "500" and then retired from racing prior to defending the next year?

(a) Kenny Brack
(b) Eddie Cheever
(c) Gil de Ferran
(d) Juan Pablo Montoya

334. In what year did Duke Nalon, driving the powerful Novi, start the race from the pole and lead the first 23 laps before a broken axle caused him to crash in turn three and be injured with serious burns?

(a) 1949
(b) 1954
(c) 1959
(d) 1964

335. The first race after the break for World War II was won by George Robson in a car that was how many years old?

(a) one year
(b) three years
(c) five years
(d) eight years

336. On the first lap of the 1958 race, the pole sitter and the second-place starter crashed together and caused a huge accident involving 15 cars and eventually eliminating eight cars. Who went over the wall but fortunately avoided serious injury?

(a) A. J. Foyt
(b) Paul Goldsmith
(c) Pat O'Connor
(d) Jerry Unser

337. In the first "500," second-place finisher Ralph Mulford stopped to change a total of 14 tires during the race, while winner Ray Harroun, who ran a more paced race, stopped and changed a total of how many tires?

    (a) two tires
    (b) four tires
    (c) eight tires
    (d) 16 tires

338. In the 1996 race, which driver set the all-time speed record for a lap in the race (236.103 mph)?

    (a) Eddie Cheever
    (b) Buddy Lazier
    (c) Arie Luyendyk
    (d) Tony Stewart

339. In 1927, defending champion Frank Lockhart was leading at 120 laps when his engine threw a connecting rod that ended his chances of becoming the first repeat winner. After getting out of his car, what did he ask for?

    (a) beer
    (b) Coke
    (c) hot dog
    (d) milk

340. Only three drivers drove in the "500" in all three of these types of cars: upright dirt car, "roadster", and rear engine. Who were they?

(a) Duane Carter Sr.
(b) Cliff Griffith
(c) Eddie Johnson
(d) Jim Rathmann
(e) Troy Ruttman
(f) Rodger Ward

341. In what year did the Speedway and Borg Warner begin presenting the "Baby Borg" to the winner? The "Baby Borg" is a 14 inch version of the big trophy valued at about $25,000.

(a) 1968
(b) 1978
(c) 1988
(d) 1998

342. In 1987, there was no more room on the Borg-Warner trophy for images of the winners. A base was added to the trophy to provide more space. The first image on the base is in gold rather than silver, and is the image of the only non-winner on the trophy. Whose image is it?

(a) Carl Fisher
(b) Tony Hulman
(c) Eddie Rickenbacker
(d) Wilbur Shaw

343. In the 1941 race, who became the first driver of a gasoline-fueled car to go the full distance with no pit stops?

    (a) Emil Andres
    (b) Cliff Bergere
    (c) Rex Mays
    (d) Paul Russo

344. In 1947, with a participants strike imminent by the American Society of Professional Automobile Racing (ASPAR, led at that time by Ralph Hepburn), who mediated a successful compromise which resulted in ten ASPAR drivers making the starting field?

    (a) Harlan Fengler
    (b) Bill Fox
    (c) Pop Myers
    (d) Wilbur Shaw

345. The 1973 race was disastrous. Which participant did not lose his life from the month of May in 1973?

    (a) Art Pollard
    (b) Swede Savage
    (c) Armando Teran
    (d) Salt Walther

346. In the 1964 race, while leading, Jimmy Clark's Dunlop tires began chunking, causing excessive vibration and, ultimately, suspension failure. His Lotus teammate withdrew from the race because of the same tire-chunking problem. Who was his teammate?

(a) Jack Brabham
(b) Dan Gurney
(c) Bobby Johns
(d) Bobby Marshman

347. In the 1964 race, Bobby Marshman jumped to a very sizable early lead then was sidelined on lap 39 by what?

(a) blown engine
(b) bottomed out, ripping out oil plug
(c) crashed
(d) lost wheel

348. The Borg-Warner trophy, which is presented to the winner, has one driver's name misspelled. Who is it?

(a) Mario Andretti
(b) Gil de Ferran
(c) Johnnie Parsons
(d) Bill Vukovich

1947 and 1948 winner Mauri Rose
in the Blue Crown Special.

Chapter 5
Cars/Engines

349. Who drove the last turbine car during practice at Indianapolis (in 1970)?

    (a) Tony Adamowicz
    (b) Al Miller
    (c) Jigger Sirois
    (d) Bruce Walkup

350. Joe Leonard's turbine dropped out of the 1968 race because of what?

    (a) $6 ball bearing caused transmission failure
    (b) broken suspension
    (c) broken fuel shaft
    (d) reduced annulus intake area

351. Nineteen fifty-four was the year in which the entire field was powered by the same engine. What engine was it?

    (a) Ford
    (b) Miller
    (c) Novi
    (d) Offenhauser

352. The powerful Novi engine was named after what?

(a) airplane
(b) bird
(c) a place in Michigan
(d) helicopter

353. The 1963 winner, Parnelli Jones, drove the Agajanian Willard Battery Special, nicknamed "Calhoun." How many years had this car been driven in the race?

(a) two
(b) three
(c) four
(d) five

354. Who was the sponsor of Eddie Cheever's winning car in 1998?

(a) Conseco
(b) Marlboro
(c) Pennzoil
(d) Rachel's Potato Chips

355. The second place finisher in 1946 was Jimmy Jackson, who had attended Arsenal Technical High School in Indianapolis and had his car painted in the school color. What color was it?

(a) blue
(b) green
(c) orange
(d) red

356. Parnelli Jones's 1967 turbine was nicknamed which two of these names?

    (a) Four Wheel Drive Freddie
    (b) Silent Sam
    (c) STP Bomber
    (d) Whooshmobile

357. Match Jim Clark's car number with the year.

    1963 (a)   #6
    1964 (b)   #19
    1965 (c)   #31
    1966 (d)   #82
    1967 (e)   #92

358. Jimmy Murphy won the 1922 race. Starting from the pole, he was the first pole winner to win the race and was also the first owner/driver to win. He dominated the race by leading 153 of the 200 laps. What type of car was he driving?

    (a) Ballot
    (b) Duesenberg
    (c) Mercedes
    (d) Stutz

359. In what year was the race first won by a front-wheel-drive car?

    (a) 1911
    (b) 1920
    (c) 1930
    (d) 1940

360. The 1932 winning car of Fred Frame was still competing in practice for the "500" in what year?

   (a) 1938
   (b) 1941
   (c) 1948
   (d) 1953

361. In 1963, which driver did not drive a Novi in the race?

   (a) Allen Crowe
   (b) Jim Hurtubise
   (c) Art Malone
   (d) Bobby Unser

362. In 1948, Duke Nalon finished the highest of any Novi in 23 years of competing at Indy. What place did he finish?

   (a) first
   (b) second
   (c) third
   (d) fourth

363. In what year did the first rear-engine car (driven by Lee Oldfield) appear at the Speedway?

   (a) 1937
   (b) 1958
   (c) 1959
   (d) 1960

364. In 1948, Billy Devore qualified 20th and finished 12th in a very unique car. What was unique about this car?

(a) two engines
(b) first car with a wing
(c) six wheels
(d) first green car at the track

365. Who crashed the 1967 turbine in practice for the 1968 race, preventing it from ever racing again?

(a) Graham Hill
(b) Joe Leonard
(c) Art Pollard
(d) Mike Spence

366. Who had the highest finish (11th) in a Novi during the years in which they were owned by the Granatelli brothers? (1961-1966)

(a) Jim Hurtubise
(b) Art Malone
(c) Jim McElreath
(d) Bobby Unser

367. What was the last year in which there were actual carburetors on a race car in the "500"?

(a) 1933
(b) 1941
(c) 1953
(d) 1963

368. Ray Harroun, the winner of the first "500," drove the Marmon Wasp to victory in 1911. What car number was the Marmon Wasp?

    (a) #1
    (b) #13
    (c) #32
    (d) #99

369. The last front-wheel-drive car to win the race did so in what year?

    (a) 1929
    (b) 1939
    (c) 1949
    (d) 1959

370. Who drove Jim Hall's "Yellow Submarine" in 1979, dropping out after having led 85 of the first 100 laps?

    (a) Johnny Rutherford
    (b) Tom Sneva
    (c) Al Unser Sr.
    (d) Bobby Unser

371. In 1984, former Formula One World Champion Emerson Fittipaldi came out of retirement to race at Indy for the first time. What color was his car?

    (a) green
    (b) orange
    (c) pink
    (d) yellow

372. In 1970, who drove J. C. Agajanian's Mongoose-Offy, which would be the first and last car to run in the "500" with a roll cage?

(a) Dick Atkins
(b) Bobby Johns
(c) Bill Vukovich Jr.
(d) Bruce Walkup

373. In the 1946 race, Paul Russo drove a very unique car. What was unique about it?

(a) six wheels
(b) eight wheels
(c) turbine engine
(d) twin engines

374. In 1963, who at the age of 50, qualified one of Mickey Thompson's "skateboard" cars?

(a) Duane Carter
(b) Dan Gurney
(c) Chuck Hulse
(d) Chuck Stevenson

375. In 1964, who attempted unsuccessfully to qualify a dirt car for the "500"? It marked the last time a dirt car would make a qualifying attempt.

(a) Bill Cheesbourg
(b) Cliff Griffith
(c) Troy Ruttman
(d) Bob Veith

376. In 1970, hard-luck driver Lloyd Ruby drove for Gene White and charged from 25th to first before an engine failure ended his race. How many engine failures did he experience in the month of May?

(a) three
(b) five
(c) seven
(d) ten

377. In 1970, Al Unser drove the Johnny Lightning Special to the win in dominating fashion. George Bignotti constructed what type of chassis for Unser?

(a) Colt
(b) Coyote
(c) Eagle
(d) Lola

378. In 1970, the year after winning the "500," Mario Andretti drove for STP and drove what kind of chassis?

(a) Eagle
(b) Lola
(c) McNamara
(d) Shrike

379. The 1972 winner Mark Donohue drove a Penske #66 McLaren. Who was his sponsor?

(a) Patrick Petroleum
(b) STP
(c) Sugaripe Prune
(d) Sunoco

380. The Judd engine was actually based on what?

(a) Chevrolet
(b) Cosworth
(c) Honda
(d) March

381. In 1980, winner Johnny Rutherford's Chaparral with ground effects was nicknamed what?

(a) Yellow Balloon
(b) Yellow Colt
(c) Yellow Missile
(d) Yellow Submarine

382. In the first "500" in 1911, how many single-seat cars were in the race?

(a) one
(b) ten
(c) 25
(d) 40

383. What driver drove the "Batmobile" in several races in the early 1980s?

(a) Geoff Brabham
(b) Howdy Holmes
(c) Danny Ongais
(d) Tim Richmond

384. Who was rookie pole winner Teo Fabi's sponsor in 1983?

(a) Kraco Car Stereo
(b) Pennzoil
(c) Skoal Bandit
(d) STP Oil Treatment

385. In 1994, Penske Racing unveiled the 209-cubic-inch turbocharged pushrod engine that dominated the race, leading 193 of 200 laps. How much horsepower did the engine generate?

(a) 600
(b) 800
(c) 900
(d) 1000

386. Starting in 1950, certain drivers had three adhesive stripes on the rear of their cars. What did the stripes signify?

(a) car experiencing mechanical problems
(b) nonqualified car
(c) overweight car
(d) rookie driver

387. Sam Hanks retired after the 1957 race, opening up George Salih's winning car. Who drove the "laid-down Offy" (actually 18 degrees from horizontal) in the 1958 race to it's second consecutive "500" victory?

(a) Jimmy Bryan
(b) A. J. Foyt
(c) Pat O'Connor
(d) Dick Rathmann

388. In 1939, Wilbur Shaw's winning car was the first of what since the winning car in 1919?

(a) foreign-built
(b) rear engine
(c) single seat
(d) six wheels

389. In 1972, who designed a radical car that incorporated dihedral wings (which were removed prior to qualifications) for the "Super Team" of Al Unser, Joe Leonard, and Mario Andretti?

(a) Dan Gurney
(b) Bruce McLaren
(c) Maurice Phillipe
(d) Roman Slobodynskj

390. Cars from what country won four of the first seven 500-mile races?

    (a) England
    (b) France
    (c) Germany
    (d) United States

391. Mike Boyle (owner) and Cotton Henning (mechanic) were responsible for bringing to Indy a very successful car that became the first to win in consecutive years. What car was it?

    (a) Alfa Romeo
    (b) Maserati
    (c) Novi
    (d) Peugeot

392. Who funded the Novi cars, which were the most powerful and fastest cars at the Speedway in the late 1940s and early 1950s?

    (a) Andy Granatelli
    (b) Lou Moore
    (c) A. J. Watson
    (d) Lou Welch

393. In the 1966 "500" there was only one front engine "roadster" that started the race. Who drove the car?

    (a) Bobby Grim
    (b) Jim Hurtubise
    (c) Eddie Johnson
    (d) Dempsey Wilson

394. In 1968, Andy Granatelli had three turbine-powered cars in the race. In Gasoline Alley, the cars were nicknamed what?

(a) doorstops
(b) hush mobiles
(c) red bombers
(d) Silent Sam II

395. By the mid 1960s, the "roadster", which had won every "500" from 1953 to 1964, was being called what?

(a) dinosaur
(b) mongoose
(c) speedster
(d) turtle

396. The 1955 winner, Bob Sweikert, drove the John Zink Special. This "roadster" was what colors?

(a) turquoise and white
(b) hunter green and white
(c) tropical rose and cream
(d) executive red and white

397. What driver finished in second place in the 1973 "500" in the Sugaripe Prune Special?

(a) Gary Bettenhausen
(b) Mel Kenyon
(c) Bud Tinglestad
(d) Bill Vukovich II

398. Jack Brabham's Cooper Climax started the modern rear-engine era in 1961. In what place did Brabham finish?

    (a) third
    (b) sixth
    (c) ninth
    (d) 22nd

399. In 2001, Helio Castroneves drove what numbered Penske car to his first Indy 500 victory?

    (a) #1
    (b) #3
    (c) #6
    (d) #68

400. In 1963, what defending Formula One champion and future Indy 500 champion decided to step out of one of Mickey Thompson's innovative "skateboard" cars after crashing in practice? He did not participate in the Indy 500 until 1966.

    (a) Jim Clark
    (b) Graham Hill
    (c) Jochen Rindt
    (d) Jackie Stewart

Sam Hanks: 1957 winner Sam Hanks
in George Salih's "sidewinder."

Chapter 6
Rules and Regulations

401. In what year was the limit for the number of starters most recently determined to be 33, primarily due to safety reasons?

    (a) 1930
    (b) 1934
    (c) 1936
    (d) 1940

402. In what year did the era of the transponder arrive at the Speedway, with transmitters attached to every car for the timing and scoring?

    (a) 1960
    (b) 1970
    (c) 1980
    (d) 1990

403. In 1930, a revision of the flag code resulted in the green flag being used to start the race. From the first "500" through 1929, which flag was used to start the race?

    (a) yellow
    (b) white
    (c) red
    (d) checkered

404. In what year did the roll bar behind the driver's head become mandatory?

    (a) 1954
    (b) 1959
    (c) 1964
    (d) 1969

405. Up until what year was the driver required to climb out of the car and re-enter during a pit stop for fuel?

    (a) 1916
    (b) 1926
    (c) 1936
    (d) 1946

406. In what year were regulations adopted that allowed a maximum of six gallons of oil to be carried on board? For the first time, oil could not be added during the race.

    (a) 1923
    (b) 1933
    (c) 1941
    (d) 1951

407. In what year was the new pit lane built, with a main straight wall separating the pits and the track for the first time? It was no longer permissible to fire the engine in the garage area and drive from Gasoline Alley through the pits and onto the track.

   (a) 1937
   (b) 1947
   (c) 1957
   (d) 1967

408. In what year were protective helmets first required for the drivers?

   (a) 1935
   (b) 1940
   (c) 1945
   (d) 1950

409. For the 1936 race, a total fuel limit of how many gallons was instituted, which happened to be the lowest fuel allowance in history? During the last ten laps of the race, four out of the top ten leaders ran out of fuel.

   (a) 37.5 gallons
   (b) 50 gallons
   (c) 102.5 gallons
   (d) 200 gallons

410. USAC (United States Auto Club) became the sanctioning body for the "500" in what year, after AAA decided to no longer be involved in motor sports?

(a) 1936
(b) 1946
(c) 1956
(d) 1966

411. In the first two "500s," five cars per row were used for the starting lineup. Then for several years, it was reduced to four cars per row. In what year was three cars per row implemented? This format has been unchanged since.

(a) 1921
(b) 1931
(c) 1946
(d) 1956

412. Pat Flaherty wore a sleeveless T-shirt for his win in what year? Fire-retardant uniforms were not mandated until 1959.

(a) 1952
(b) 1954
(c) 1956
(d) 1958

413. In what year was the caution period pacer light system retired and the pack-up rule initiated?

    (a) 1976
    (b) 1979
    (c) 1982
    (d) 1985

414. In 1972, what driver was leading the race on lap 188 when a punctured tire very well may have cost him victory? He pitted in his teammate's pit stall, was serviced by his teammate's crew (which eventually caused a penalty), resulting in a 12th place finish rather than his second-place finish on the track.

    (a) Gary Bettenhausen
    (b) Jerry Grant
    (c) Mike Mosley
    (d) Swede Savage

415. In what year was a rule implemented making a minimum of two pit stops a requirement?

    (a) 1945
    (b) 1955
    (c) 1965
    (d) 1975

416. After the fiery tragedy of May 1973, rules changed, and carrying 75 gallons of fuel on board the car was no longer allowed. What was the maximum amount of fuel allowed on board in a fuel cell on the left side of the car?

    (a) 20 gallons
    (b) 30 gallons
    (c) 40 gallons
    (d) 50 gallons

417. What "500" winner had several run-ins with race officials and was eventually not permitted to compete at the Indianapolis Motor Speedway?

    (a) Billy Arnold
    (b) Fred Frame
    (c) Lou Moore
    (d) Louis Schneider

418. In 1920, a procedure was established in which a driver would raise his hand coming to the start/finish line to begin a qualification attempt. What was the last year this procedure would be used before the task of signaling fell to a team representative?

    (a) 1953
    (b) 1963
    (c) 1973
    (d) 1983

419. Former chief steward Harlan Fengler drove in the "500" and was a riding mechanic as well, but what was his trademark as chief steward?

    (a) cigar
    (b) pipe
    (c) red hat
    (d) yellow jacket

420. In 1912, AAA established a safety formula that determined how many cars should compete in a racing event. The formula stated that one car should be allotted per specified length of racing surface. For the 2.5-mile track at Indianapolis, it worked out to thirty-three cars. What was the distance?

    (a) 100 feet
    (b) 200 feet
    (c) 300 feet
    (d) 400 feet

421. Riding mechanics were not mandatory in 1911. From 1912 to 1922, riding mechanics were mandatory. Then, from 1923 to 1929, they were not mandatory. From 1930 to what year were riding mechanics mandatory for the last time?

    (a) 1933
    (b) 1937
    (c) 1941
    (d) 1946

422. In 1926, with Frank Lockhart leading by more than thirty seconds at 380 miles, it began to rain. At 400 miles, he was declared the winner as rain fell hard. The rule at the time required how many miles be completed in order for the race to be considered official?

(a) 100 miles
(b) 251 miles
(c) 350 miles
(d) 500 miles

423. From 1930 to 1935, nine drivers and six riding mechanics were fatally injured, prompting what program to be established?

(a) bladders for fuel tanks
(b) rookie tests for all new drivers
(c) installation of soft walls
(d) pack up behind pace car

424. In 1937, what type of inspection was incorporated on all vital car parts to hopefully disclose flaws and improve safety?

(a) Magnaflux
(b) ultrasound
(c) visual
(d) x-ray

425. For the first several years, the starting positions in the race were determined by the date on which each entry was received. What year was the first in which cars were lined up in order of qualifying speed?

   (a) 1915
   (b) 1920
   (c) 1925
   (d) 1930

426. For the 1930 race, the president of the Speedway, Eddie Rickenbacker, decided to increase the engine size significantly and to require the cars to be two-seaters in an attempt to entice the passenger-car manufacturers back to the "500" to compete. The period was sometime referred to as what?

   (a) dream car era
   (b) "junk" era
   (c) "roadster" era
   (d) speedster era

427. In what year did the use of seat belts become mandatory?

   (a) 1933
   (b) 1946
   (c) 1953
   (d) 1963

428. In 1938, one change of the regulations was that there were no restrictions on the kind of fuel used. At the time, a typical car ran nine miles on a gallon of gasoline, while cars got how many miles on a gallon of alcohol, which had a tendency to allow the engines to run cooler?

(a) three miles
(b) six miles
(c) 12 miles
(d) 18 miles

429. In what year was a qualification attempt changed from ten laps to four laps? It has remained there ever since.

(a) 1919
(b) 1939
(c) 1959
(d) 1979

In 1967, Parnelli Jones's revolutionary STP turbine
drops out with three laps remaining and a huge lead.

Chapter 7
Qualifications

430. In 1985, there were two Buick V-6 engines in the race; one started on the pole, and one started in the middle of the first row. Pancho Carter sat on the pole. Who started second?

    (a) Scott Brayton
    (b) Jim Crawford
    (c) Derek Daly
    (d) Tom Sneva

431. Match their top qualifying position with each driver.

Milka Duno	(a) fourth
Sarah Fisher	(b) sixth
Janet Guthrie	(c) ninth
Danica Patrick	(d) 14th
Lyn St. James	(e) 27th

432. What rookie in 1969 nearly won the pole, but waved off a potential pole-qualifying attempt?

    (a) Mark Donohue
    (b) George Follmer
    (c) Peter Revson
    (d) Jigger Sirois

433. Howdy Holmes raced in six "500s" and took the checkered flag in each. What was his highest starting position?

   (a) second
   (b) ninth
   (c) 14th
   (d) 17th

434. Nineteen eighty-three saw the first rookie since Walt Faulkner in 1950 win the pole. Who was it?

   (a) Derek Daly
   (b) Teo Fabi
   (c) Chris Kneifel
   (d) Al Unser Jr.

435. Rick Mears has the record for pole starts. How many?

   (a) four times
   (b) five times
   (c) six times
   (d) seven times

436. In 1995, what race team failed to qualify for the first time since competing at Indy?

   (a) Foyt Racing
   (b) Ganassi Racing
   (c) Penske Racing
   (d) Rahal/Letterman Racing

437. Name the first second-generation driver to qualify for the "500."

    (a) Gary Bettenhausen
    (b) Billy Devore
    (c) Johnny Parsons
    (d) Billy Vukovich

438. In 1980, Jerry Sneva qualified for his best starting position in any "500" for which he had qualified. What was his starting position?

    (a) fifth
    (b) 16th
    (c) 21st
    (d) 26th

439. In 1994, Lyn St. James made her best qualification at Indy. What was her starting position?

    (a) fourth
    (b) sixth
    (c) ninth
    (d) 13th

440. In 1980, Spike Gelhausen qualified for his best "500" starting position. What was it?

    (a) fourth
    (b) 12th
    (c) 16th
    (d) 23rd

441. Johnny Rutherford won the 1974 race from what starting position?

   (a) 22nd
   (b) 25th
   (c) 28th
   (d) 33rd

442. In what year did Jim Hurtubise last qualify his front-engine Mallard, signifying the final time a front-engine car would qualify for the "500"?

   (a) 1966
   (b) 1967
   (c) 1968
   (d) 1969

443. Rank the starting positions with the highest number of wins in descending order.

   (a) first
   (b) second
   (c) third
   (d) fourth
   (e) fifth

444. In 1971, what driver qualified with three laps at 52.45 seconds and one lap at 52.44, resulting in the most consistent qualifying run in history at the time?

   (a) Mario Andretti
   (b) Jim Malloy
   (c) Peter Revson
   (d) George Snider

445. What former winner bumped his way into the 2008 "500" field with less than ten minutes left on Bump Day?

(a) Sam Hornish Jr.
(b) Buddy Lazier
(c) Buddy Rice
(d) Dan Wheldon

446. In 1979, a controversy involving the turbo pop-off valve resulted in an extra qualifying session the day before the race. As a result, how many cars started the race?

(a) 33 cars
(b) 35 cars
(c) 37 cars
(d) 40 cars

447. In 1963, the second-place finisher from the 1962 race failed to qualify. Who was it?

(a) Masten Gregory
(b) Pedro Rodriguez
(c) Len Sutton
(d) Jack Turner

448. In 1970, driving yellow car #18 for Pat Patrick, what driver missed taking the pole from eventual winner Al Unser by 0.003 seconds?

(a) Mark Donohue
(b) Dan Gurney
(c) Mike Mosley
(d) Johnny Rutherford

449. In 1991, what fan favorite qualified on the second day of qualifications and actually exceeded the pole speed of Rick Mears?

(a) Gary Bettenhausen
(b) Pancho Carter
(c) Jim Crawford
(d) Roberto Guerrero

450. From 1933 to 1938, how many laps constituted a qualifying run?

(a) three laps
(b) five laps
(c) ten laps
(d) 20 laps

1977 winner A. J. Foyt with his Coyote becomes the first four-time winner of the Indy 500.

Chapter 8
Records

451. In what year did the total purse exceed $1,000,000 for the first time?

    (a) 1961
    (b) 1966
    (c) 1971
    (d) 1976

452. Who was the third driver in history to win the "500" in consecutive years?

    (a) Helio Castroneves
    (b) Mauri Rose
    (c) Al Unser
    (d) Bill Vukovich

453. Who was the second two-time winner of the Indianapolis 500?

    (a) Billy Arnold
    (b) Louis Meyer
    (c) Mauri Rose
    (d) Wilbur Shaw

454. On race day in 1981, Mary Fendrich Hulman was ill and in the hospital. As a result, she was not able to give the starting command. Who replaced her that day and gave the command of "Gentlemen, start your engines"?

    (a) Joe Cloutier
    (b) John Cooper
    (c) Mari Hulman George
    (d) Tony George

455. In 2006, public address announcer, Tom Carnegie, called his last race. How many consecutive races did he call?

    (a) 31
    (b) 41
    (c) 51
    (d) 61

456. In 1972, the pole winner exceeded the previous track record by over 17 mph. Who broke Peter Revson's track record, claiming both the record and the pole?

    (a) Gary Bettenhausen
    (b) Mark Donohue
    (c) Peter Revson
    (d) Bobby Unser

457. The official record for qualifying at Indy was set in 1996, when the record run was a 236.986 mph average. The car/driver did not win the pole, as he was a second-day qualifier. Who set the record?

(a) Scott Brayton
(b) Pancho Carter
(c) Roberto Guerrero
(d) Arie Luyendyk

458. Match the number of laps led at the "500" with the driver.

Mario Andretti	(a) 555
Ralph DePalma	(b) 556
A. J. Foyt	(c) 612
Al Unser Sr.	(d) 644

459. Match the closest finishes in "500" history (in seconds) with the drivers.

Al Unser Jr. and Scott Goodyear	(a) 0.0430
Gil de Ferran and Helio Castroneves	(b) 0.0635
Gordon Johncock and Rick Mears	(c) 0.1600
Sam Hornish Jr. and Marco Andretti	(d) 0.2990

460. The first driver to earn more than $50,000 for winning was who and in what year?

(a) Wilbur Shaw, 1937
(b) Kelly Petillo, 1935
(c) Bill Cummings, 1934
(d) Billy Arnold, 1930

461. A. J. Foyt holds the record for driving in the most Indy "500s." How many?

    (a) 28
    (b) 31
    (c) 35
    (d) 37

462. Who was the oldest winner of the race at 47 years and 360 days?

    (a) A. J. Foyt
    (b) Eddie Cheever
    (c) Sam Hanks
    (d) Al Unser Sr.

463. Who won the first race in the history of the Indy Racing League, run at Orlando-Disney World in 1996?

    (a) Buzz Calkins
    (b) Roberto Guerrero
    (c) Arie Luyendyk
    (d) Tony Stewart

464. Who was the third driver to become a three-time winner of the "500"?

    (a) A. J. Foyt
    (b) Mauri Rose
    (c) Wilbur Shaw
    (d) Al Unser

465. At 57 years old, who was the oldest driver to compete in the "500"?

(a) Mario Andretti
(b) Ralph Hepburn
(c) A. J. Foyt
(d) Al Unser Sr.

466. Bill Kennedy Jr. attended 56 consecutive "500s" before the health of his wife, Fran, caused him to miss in 1989. In what year was Bill Kennedy a rookie?

(a) 1920
(b) 1925
(c) 1930
(d) 1935

467. In 2008, the winner of the race also accomplished the most consistent qualifying performance in history, eclipsing George Snider's run of 1971. The difference between the four qualifying laps was 0.0049 mph. Who did it?

(a) Helio Castroneves
(b) Scott Dixon
(c) Tony Kanaan
(d) Dan Wheldon

468. Who was the first four-time winner of the "500"?

(a) A. J. Foyt
(b) Rick Mears
(c) Louis Meyer
(d) Al Unser Sr.

469. What driver drove the first rear-engine car in the "500"?

(a) George Bailey, 1939
(b) Jack Brabham, 1961
(c) Masten Gregory, 1965
(d) Dan Gurney, 1962

470. In 1990, Arie Luyendyk set a new race record for a speed average of almost what?

(a) 166 mph
(b) 176 mph
(c) 186 mph
(d) 196 mph

471. What "500" winner was the first to average over 100 mph for the race?

(a) Ralph DePalma
(b) Peter DePaolo
(c) Louis Meyer
(d) Fred Frame

472. In 1954, race day brought very hot weather, which resulted in a record number of drivers (both primary and relief drivers) driving one car. How many drivers drove Art Cross's 11th place-finishing car that day?

(a) two
(b) three
(c) four
(d) five

473. Driving in his fourth "500," who, at 22 years old, became the youngest winner of the "500"?

(a) Helio Castroneves
(b) Parnelli Jones
(c) Rick Mears
(d) Troy Ruttman

474. Who were the first and only pair of brothers to win the "500"?

(a) Mario and Aldo Andretti
(b) Gary and Tony Bettenhausen
(c) Tom and Jerry Sneva
(d) Bobby and Al Unser

475. Helio Castroneves, the winner of the 2009 race, won a record prize. How much?

(a) $2,048,005
(b) $2,548,005
(c) $3,048,005
(d) $3,548,005

476. A. J. Foyt leads with thirty-five 500-mile race starts. Who is next, with 29?

(a) Mario Andretti
(b) Gordon Johncock
(c) Johnny Rutherford
(d) Al Unser Sr.

477. In 1931, Dave Evans drove the Cummins Diesel Special, finishing 13th nearly 38 minutes behind the winner, Louis Schneider. He accomplished a very unique feat. Which was it?

(a) He led every lap in the race but the last ten.
(b) He used five different relief drivers.
(c) He started last (42nd) and finished 13th.
(d) He completed the race without a pit stop.

478. To date, two second-generation "500" racers have won. Who are they?

(a) Michael Andretti
(b) Buddy Lazier
(c) Al Unser Jr.
(d) Bill Vukovich Jr.

479. In what year was the Rookie of the Year award presented for the first time?

(a) 1946
(b) 1952
(c) 1958
(d) 1964

480. In 1980, Jim McElreath qualified in 11th position, making him the oldest driver to ever have made the race at the time. How old was he?

(a) 48
(b) 50
(c) 52
(d) 54

481. In 1936, what driver started a remarkable streak of top-four finishes in nine consecutive races?

   (a) Ted Horn
   (b) Rex Mays
   (c) Louis Meyer
   (d) Wilbur Shaw

482. Who was the first woman to qualify for the Indy "500"?

   (a) Sarah Fisher
   (b) Janet Guthrie
   (c) Danica Patrick
   (d) Lyn St. James

483. Who, in 1965, gave the front-engine "roadster" its last victory in USAC competition?

   (a) Don Branson
   (b) A. J. Foyt
   (c) Parnelli Jones
   (d) Rodger Ward

484. Who was the second woman to ever race in the "500"?

   (a) Sarah Fisher
   (b) Danica Patrick
   (c) Lyn St. James
   (d) Desiré Wilson

485. Who was the first two-time "500" winner?

(a) Louis Meyer
(b) Tommy Milton
(c) Wilbur Shaw
(d) Mauri Rose

486. Who won the inaugural Ontario California 500 in 1970?

(a) Mario Andretti
(b) Joe Leonard
(c) Jim McElreath
(d) Al Unser

487. In the first "500," Ray Harroun's average speed for the race was just under what?

(a) 55 mph
(b) 65 mph
(c) 75 mph
(d) 85 mph

488. Who became a track celebrity by being the first fan in line for the track to open from 1950 to 1984?

(a) Larry Biancho
(b) Larry Bisceglia
(c) Ralph Liguori
(d) Dempsey Wilson

489. Who was the first three-time winner of the Indianapolis "500"?

(a) Louis Meyer
(b) Tommy Milton
(c) Mauri Rose
(d) Wilbur Shaw

490. Nineteen eighty-four has the distinction of having the record for most entries. How many?

(a) 55
(b) 69
(c) 91
(d) 117

491. In 2000, a rookie won the race for the first time since Graham Hill in 1966. Who was it?

(a) Marco Andretti
(b) Helio Castroneves
(c) Sam Hornish Jr.
(d) Juan Pablo Montoya

492. Match these race winners with their starting positions, which happen to be the four lowest starting positions for any winner.

Fred Frame, 1932	(a) 25th
Ray Harroun, 1911	(b) 27th
Louis Meyer, 1936	(c) 28th
Johnny Rutherford, 1974	(d) 28th

493. What was the first year in which rain caused the race to be run over two days?

(a) 1950
(b) 1967
(c) 1986
(d) 2004

494. What was the first year ever in which the "500" was stopped by a red flag due to an accident?

(a) 1958
(b) 1964
(c) 1966
(d) 1973

495. During the 1964 season, how many victories did A. J. Foyt secure on his way to his fourth national championship?

(a) seven of 13 races
(b) eight of 13 races
(c) nine of 13 races
(d) ten of 13 races

496. Who was the first driver to officially break the 150-mph barrier?

(a) A. J. Foyt
(b) Jim Hurtubise
(c) Parnelli Jones
(d) Rodger Ward

497. Nineteen sixteen had the smallest starting field in the history of the race. How many cars?

(a) 21
(b) 24
(c) 26
(d) 27

498. In 1954, who became the first driver to officially break the 140-mph barrier?

(a) Art Cross
(b) Sam Hanks
(c) Jack McGrath
(d) Bill Vukovich

499. Who was the first woman to compete in an Indy car race at any track?

(a) Janet Guthrie
(b) Arlene Hiss
(c) Lyn St. James
(d) Desiré Wilson

500. In 1977, who was the first driver to officially break the 200-mph barrier?

(a) Mario Andretti
(b) A. J. Foyt
(c) Danny Ongais
(d) Tom Sneva

501. For the 1989 race, the entire track had been newly paved, resulting in an increase in the field's average qualifying speed by how much?

    (a) four mph
    (b) six mph
    (c) eight mph
    (d) ten mph

502. Who was the second four-time winner of the "500"?

    (a) Emerson Fittipaldi
    (b) Johnny Rutherford
    (c) Al Unser Sr.
    (d) Bobby Unser

503. Starting with the inaugural "500" in 1911, what was the first "500" in which no relief drivers were used?

    (a) 1930
    (b) 1941
    (c) 1952
    (d) 1963

504. What father-son combination was the first to attempt to qualify at Indy?

    (a) Mario and Michael Andretti
    (b) Jack and Geoff Brabham
    (c) Jim and James McElreath
    (d) Al and Al Unser Jr.

505. Which winner was the first to receive more than $100,000 for winning?

(a) A. J. Foyt, 1961
(b) Sam Hanks, 1957
(c) Bob Sweikert, 1955
(d) Rodger Ward, 1959

506. In 1984, Chris Kneifel became the first driver since 1929 to start the "500" under what circumstance?

(a) first alternate starter
(b) driver of a six-wheeled car
(c) driver of a three-wheeled car
(d) riding mechanic

507. In what year was the shortest official race in history?

(a) 1950
(b) 1973
(c) 1975
(d) 1976

508. In what year was the 500-mile race heard on the radio in its entirety for the first time?

(a) 1941
(b) 1953
(c) 1957
(d) 1963

509. In what year was the race actually scheduled for less than 500 miles? (300 miles)

    (a) 1916
    (b) 1919
    (c) 1941
    (d) 1946

510. In 1996, the first year of the Indy Racing League, the most number of rookies started the race since 19 in 1930. How many rookies started in 1996?

    (a) 12
    (b) 14
    (c) 15
    (d) 17

511. In 1970, what driver led 1,527 laps during the USAC season, with the next lap leader at 130 laps?

    (a) Mario Andretti
    (b) A. J. Foyt
    (c) Joe Leonard
    (d) Al Unser

512. In 1990, pole winner Emerson Fittipaldi set a record for the greatest number of consecutive laps led from the start before finally relinquishing. The old record was 81 laps by Frank Lockhart in 1927. How many did Fittipaldi lead before finally giving way to another driver?

(a) 92 laps
(b) 102 laps
(c) 112 laps
(d) 122 laps

513. Who was the first Canadian to win an Indy 500?

(a) Billy Foster
(b) Scott Goodyear
(c) Paul Tracy
(d) Jacques Villeneuve

514. In 1994, a first occurred when a driver competed in the Indy 500 and the World 600 in Charlotte, NC on the same day. Who was he?

(a) John Andretti
(b) Jeff Gordon
(c) Robby Gordon
(d) Tony Stewart

515. In 2003, Roger Penske tied whose record, which had stood for more than half a century, by fielding the winning car for three straight years?

   (a) J. C. Agajanian
   (b) Mike Boyle
   (c) Harry Miller
   (d) Lou Moore

516. Who was the first and only driver to date to win the Indy 500 in each of his first two attempts?

   (a) Helio Castroneves
   (b) Louis Meyer
   (c) Wilbur Shaw
   (d) Bill Vukovich

517. In 1952, who was the first Rookie of the Year award winner?

   (a) Alberto Ascari
   (b) Art Cross
   (c) Jim Rathmann
   (d) Bob Sweikert

518. Who was the first woman to drive the pace car for the start of the "500"?

   (a) Mari Hulman George
   (b) Janet Guthrie
   (c) Elaine Irwin-Mellencamp
   (d) Dinah Shore

519. Who was the first driver to win the "500" in consecutive years? He also happened to drive the same car each year.

    (a) Tommy Milton
    (b) Mauri Rose
    (c) Wilbur Shaw
    (d) Bill Vukovich

520. What driver was able to complete 1,799 out of a possible 1,800 laps in nine consecutive starts from the 1936 race to the 1948 race?

    (a) Emil Andres
    (b) Ted Horn
    (c) Rex Mays
    (d) Louis Meyer

521. Who led the first lap in the history of the Indianapolis 500?

    (a) Johnny Aitken
    (b) Joe Dawson
    (c) Ray Harroun
    (d) Ralph Mulford

522. Who was the first "500" winner to drive the entire race without a relief driver?

    (a) Joe Dawson, 1912
    (b) Jules Goux, 1913
    (c) Ray Harroun, 1911
    (d) Rene Thomas, 1914

523. In what year did the most cars start the "500" (42 cars)?

   (a) 1911
   (b) 1922
   (c) 1933
   (d) 1946

524. In 1934, the cars were limited to a total of how many gallons of fuel to run the race?

   (a) 45 gallons
   (b) 65 gallons
   (c) 85 gallons
   (d) 105 gallons

525. Who was the first foreign winning driver since Dario Resta in 1916?

   (a) Jack Brabham
   (b) Jimmy Clark
   (c) Juan Manual Fangio
   (d) Graham Hill

526. In the entire history of the "500," how many times was a relief driver used on the winning car?

   (a) three times
   (b) six times
   (c) nine times
   (d) 12 times

527. Who is the only driver to lead the race in each of his first seven starts in the Indy 500?

(a) Mario Andretti
(b) Michael Andretti
(c) Helio Castroneves
(d) Tony Kanaan

528. Who had the largest winning margin (more than 13 minutes) over the second-place finisher?

(a) Billy Arnold, 1930
(b) Jimmy Clark, 1965
(c) Jules Goux, 1913
(d) Bill Vukovich, 1953

529. What family has the distinction of being the only one credited with three generations (father, son, and grandson) to win Rookie of the Year award?

(a) Andretti
(b) Foyt
(c) Unser
(d) Vukovich

Chapter 9
Green/White/Checker

530. Match the winning driver with their relief driver.

    Joe Dawson   (a) Norm Batten
    Peter DePaolo   (b) Don Herr
    Ray Harroun   (c) Cyrus Patschke
    Tommy Milton   (d) Howdy Wilcox

531. The original Speedway Museum was opened at 16th and Georgetown Road in 1956. Who was the curator of the museum?

    (a) Al Bloemker
    (b) Floyd Clymer
    (c) Karl Kizer
    (d) Joe Quinn

532. Joe Leonard, the near winner in 1968 and third place finisher in 1967 and 1972, was nicknamed what?

    (a) Jersey Joe
    (b) Joltin Joe
    (c) Pelican Joe
    (d) Racin Joe

533. Name two winning drivers whose faces appear on the Borg-Warner trophy, but never led a lap in the "500"?

    (a) Joe Boyer
    (b) Lora Corum
    (c) Floyd Davis
    (d) Floyd Roberts

534. In 1963 this popular driver spun late in the race in the south chute without contact and was able to resume. A short time later, he lost a wheel and crashed in the north chute. He walked back to the pits rolling his lost wheel and received a tremendous ovation. Who was this driver?

    (a) Jim Hurtubise
    (b) Bobby Marshman
    (c) Lloyd Ruby
    (d) Eddie Sachs

535. What "500" winner drove his car to victory supposedly with a crack in the engine block that had been discovered by his crew prior to the start of the race?

    (a) Mario Andretti
    (b) Buddy Lazier
    (c) Louis Meyer
    (d) Johnnie Parsons

536. Match the winning driver with his winning car number.

Mario Andretti	(a) two
Jim Clark	(b) five
Mark Donohue	(c) 14
Graham Hill	(d) 20
Gordon Johncock	(e) 24
Buddy Lazier	(f) 27
Troy Ruttman	(g) 66
Tom Sneva	(h) 82
Jacques Villeneuve	(i) 91
Bill Vukovich	(j) 98

537. Who did Rick Mears run into the back of, who was impeding his progress, as he was flying down the pit lane to make his final stop in 1982?

(a) Chip Ganassi
(b) Jim Hickman
(c) Herm Johnson
(d) Don Whittington

538. A second event was scheduled for September 9 of what year? The event was called the Harvest Day Classic and races of 25 miles, 50 miles and 100 miles were run. The same driver won all three events.

(a) 1916
(b) 1919
(c) 1922
(d) 1925

539. Up until what year were there no grandstands behind the pits?

(a) 1919
(b) 1928
(c) 1937
(d) 1946

540. Who was the only driver to finish second three times and never win the "500"?

(a) Roberto Guerrero
(b) Dan Gurney
(c) Harry Hartz
(d) Rex Mays

541. In what year did the rookie drivers put streamers on their goggles so other drivers would be aware they were rookies? The next year the use of rookie stripes on the back of the rookie's car until he passed the rookie test would be implemented.

(a) 1929
(b) 1939
(c) 1949
(d) 1959

542. In 1950, the "500" was for the first time included in the World Driving Championship. The "500" was included in the World Championship until what year?

    (a) 1954
    (b) 1956
    (c) 1958
    (d) 1960

543. The Stark & Wetzel Rookie of the Year Award was first given in 1952. Who was the first recipient?

    (a) Larry Crockett
    (b) Art Cross
    (c) Jimmy Daywalt
    (d) Al Herman

544. In 1955 a very windy day on the first day of qualifications resulted in the race teams making a general agreement not to go out for qualification attempts. Adherence to this would make the following day "pole day".
    What driver, unaware of the agreement, made a late attempt and stole the pole position?

    (a) Tony Bettenahusen
    (b) Jerry Hoyt
    (c) Jack McGrath
    (d) Bill Vukovich

545. What was 1956 winner "Pat" Flaherty's real first name?

    (a) Francis
    (b) George
    (c) Padraig
    (d) William

546. Rodger Ward's first "500" win came in 1959. How old was Ward at the time of his first victory?

    (a) 28 years old
    (b) 33 years old
    (c) 38 years old
    (d) 43 years old

547. Smokey Yunick entered his "sidecar" in 1964. Who was his driver who spun and hit the wall prior to taking the green flag attempting to qualify?

    (a) Paul Goldsmith
    (b) Masten Gregory
    (c) Bobby Johns
    (d) Al Miller

548. Whose team car was Mike Spence testing when he was fatally injured in early May 1968?

    (a) Graham Hill
    (b) Joe Leonard
    (c) Art Pollard
    (d) Greg Weld

549. For the 1969 race, the new Vel's Parnelli Jones Racing Team had bought the assets from what team?

 (a) J.C. Agajanian
 (b) John Mecom
 (c) Al Retzloff
 (d) Bob Wilke

550. In the 1971 "500" Steve Krisiloff blew an engine and hit the turn three wall. Mel Kenyon spun in the oil and hit the wall as well. As Kenyon was exiting his car he was hit by whom? Fortunately Kenyon was not injured in the close call which left tire marks on his helmet.

 (a) Mario Andretti
 (b) Wally Dallenbach
 (c) Gordon Johncock
 (d) Sammy Sessions

551. In 1972, Art Pollard crashed his qualified car and sustained a broken leg. Who replaced him in the STP Oil Treatment Special and finished 15th?

 (a) Wally Dallenbach
 (b) Steve Krisiloff
 (c) Graham McRae
 (d) Swede Savage

552. Who replaced Joe Leonard on the Vel's Parnelli Jones Team after he sustained a career ending leg injury in a crash during the Ontario 500 in March of 1974?

    (a) Mike Hiss
    (b) David Hobbs
    (c) Danny Ongais
    (d) Jan Opperman

553. In 1978 Jim Hurtubise protested the qualification procedure and ended up running on the track while Bob Harkey was beginning a qualification run. What driver actually tackled Hurtubise, who was then escorted from the area by the State Police? Hurtubise was back at the Speedway in 1979 in good graces but failed to qualify.

    (a) Jerry Karl
    (b) John Mahler
    (c) John Martin
    (d) Dick Simon

554. In 1981, Mario Andretti switched from the Penske Team to the Patrick Team. Who joined Bobby Unser and Rick Mears on the Penske Team for the 1981 "500"?

    (a) Bill Alsup
    (b) Kevin Cogan
    (c) Tom Sneva
    (d) Al Unser

555. Of the following great "500" champions, who was the only one to win Rookie of the Year?

   (a) A.J. Foyt
   (b) Rick Mears
   (c) Al Unser
   (d) Bobby Unser

556. In 1960, rookie Jim Hurtubise set records for one lap and four lap average on the final day of qualifying. He nearly hit the 150 mph barrier, and eclipsed pole sitter Eddie Sach's speed by 2.5 mph. Who was the sponsor of Hurtubise car?

   (a) Demler
   (b) Hotel Tropicana
   (c) Jim Robbins
   (d) Travelon Trailer

557. Mario Andretti competed in every "500" from 1965 through 1994 with the exception of one race. In what year did Mario not compete because of a Formula One commitment?

   (a) 1977
   (b) 1978
   (c) 1979
   (d) 1980

558. Who was the youngest pole winner in history?

   (a) Mario Andretti
   (b) Parnelli Jones
   (c) Rex Mays
   (d) Rick Mears

559. Who was the oldest pole winner in history?

    (a) Cliff Bergere
    (b) A.J. Foyt
    (c) Rick Mears
    (d) Eddie Sachs

560. Match the driver with mph barrier that he was the first to officially break.

Jim Clark	(a)	140
Roberto Guerrero	(b)	150
Graham Hill	(c)	160
Parnelli Jones	(d)	170
Jack McGrath	(e)	180
Rick Mears	(f)	190
Tom Sneva	(g)	200
Tom Sneva	(h)	210
Bobby Unser	(i)	220
Bill Vukovich Jr.	(j)	230

561. Who was the only driver in history to start from the front row in six consecutive "500's"?

    (a) Ralph DePalma
    (b) A.J. Foyt
    (c) Rex Mays
    (d) Rick Mears

562. What driver was the son of a New York Metropolitan Opera Star?

(a) Eddie Cheever
(b) Dan Gurney
(c) Peter Revson
(d) Swede Savage

563. From the first race through the 1956 "500" there was one pace lap prior to the start. In 1957 a parade lap was added to the pace lap. In what year was a second parade lap added to the pace lap prior to the green flag start?

(a) 1964
(b) 1974
(c) 1984
(d) 1994

564. The 1937 "500" was the last race that riding mechanics were mandatory. The entry form included terminology making riding mechanics optional through what year?

(a) 1948
(b) 1953
(c) 1958
(d) 1963

565. What driver was largely responsible for Colin Chapman making the trip to the Speedway in 1962? During this visit Chapman saw the potential and the opportunity the Indianapolis 500 presented.

(a) Jack Brabham
(b) Jim Clark
(c) Dan Gurney
(d) Graham Hill

566. What multiple winner has the longest time period between his first and last win?

(a) A.J. Foyt
(b) Gordon Johncock
(c) Al Unser Sr.
(d) Bobby Unser

567. Match the driver with the number of laps led in his victory year. These represent the fewest laps led for winners in history.

Gaston Chevrolet	(a) two laps
Joe Dawson	(b) ten laps
Mark Donohue	(c) 11 laps
Graham Hill	(d) 13 laps
Bobby Unser (1975)	(e) 14 laps
Jacques Villeneuve	(f) 15 laps

568. Who was largely responsible for the establishment of the Lap Prize Fund in 1920, which paid $100 for each lap led?

    (a) Eloise "Dolly" Dallenbach
    (b) Carl Fisher
    (c) Theodore "Pop" Myers
    (d) Frank Wheeler

569. What famous driver was launched over the wall in the 1931 "500", then returned to the pits, and later drove relief in his team car?

    (a) Billy Arnold
    (b) Louis Meyer
    (c) Mauri Rose
    (d) Wilbur Shaw

570. What former winner was largely responsible for the idea of presenting the winner with the pace car (or a reasonable facsimile) starting in 1936?

    (a) Billy Arnold
    (b) Peter DePaolo
    (c) Fred Frame
    (d) Tommy Milton

571. Who was the crew chief on Jim Rathmann's winning car in 1960 and Len Sutton's runner-up car in 1962?

    (a) George Bignotti
    (b) Chickie Hirashima
    (c) Smokey Yunick
    (d) A.J. Watson

572. Who was the first employee hired by USAC in 1955?

   (a) Henry Banks
   (b) Charlie Brockman
   (c) John Cooper
   (d) Frankie Delroy

573. Prior to her racing career, what was Janet Guthrie's profession?

   (a) aerospace engineer
   (b) high school teacher
   (c) mechanical engineer
   (d) psychiatrist

574. What was the last year the entire "500" field was made up of American drivers?

   (a) 1952
   (b) 1962
   (c) 1972
   (d) 1982

575. On the first turn of the first lap of the 1987 "500", what driver lost control of his car in the first turn and gently tagged eventual winner Al Unser Sr. from behind? Unser's car was fortunately not damaged.

   (a) Scott Brayton
   (b) Ludwig Heimrath, Jr.
   (c) Josele Garza
   (d) Roberto Guerrero

576. In what year was the number of warm-up laps on a qualification attempt reduced from three to two to speed up the qualification process?

(a) 1972
(b) 1977
(c) 1982
(d) 1989

577. What former Rookie of the Year had the nickname "Turtle"?

(a) Fabrizio Barbazza
(b) Phil Giebler
(c) Jim Hickman
(d) Randy Lanier

578. In 1993 Dale Coyne Racing entered a car with sponsorship from the Marmon Group. The car had a yellow and black paint scheme with the number 32 similar to the Marmon Wasp driven by Ray Harroun. Who was the driver of this entry?

(a) Eric Bachelart
(b) Dominic Dobson
(c) Stephan Gregoire
(d) Didier Theys

579. A.J. Foyt surprised the racing world on Pole Day 1993 with his retirement announcement after his teammate had crashed. Who was his teammate that prompted Foyt's retirement?

   (a) John Andretti
   (b) Eddie Cheever
   (c) Robby Gordon
   (d) Brian Herta

580. What rookie in 2000 qualified a car called the Sumar Special with a similar paint scheme (blue and white) as the Sumar Special of the 1950's?

   (a) Airton Dare'
   (b) Andy Hillenburg
   (c) Sam Hornish
   (d) Jason Leffler

581. In 2002, with just over a lap remaining Paul Tracy made a move to take the lead from Helio Castroneves. An accident between Buddy Lazier and another driver just prior to the pass nullified the overtake. Who was the other driver involved in the accident?

   (a) George Mack
   (b) Max Papis
   (c) Laurent Redon
   (d) Rick Treadway

1980 winner Johnny Rutherford in Jim Hall's
Chaparral, the "Yellow Submarine".

Chapter 10
Answers

1 (b) David

2 (d) 14 years

3 (b) Sam Hanks

4 (d) sheep farmer

5 (d) Willy T. Ribbs, 1991

6 (a) Kenny Brack

7 (c) milkman

8 (a) Billy Arnold

9 (c) Al Unser

10 (d) Scott Sharp

11 (d) Johnny Rutherford

12 (c) Paul Russo

13 Rick Mears: (a) Bakersfield, CA

   Bobby Rahal: (e) Medina, OH

   Danny Sullivan: (c) Louisville, KY

   Salt Walther: (b) Dayton, OH

   Danny Ongais: (d) Maui Island, HI

14 (a) Sarah Fisher

   (c) Lyn St. James

15 (d) Plano, TX

16 (d) Danny Sullivan

17 (d) Jack Turner

18 (b) Bill Holland

19 (a) Josele Garza

20 (c) stuntman

21 (c) Pat Flaherty

22 (c) P. J. Jones, in the red, white, and blue #98

23 (a) Aldo Andretti

24 (b) England

25 (c) Al Loquasto

26 (b) Rathmanns

27 (b) Scott Brayton, 1996

28 (d) Trieste, Italy

29 (b) A. J. Foyt

30 (c) Hiro Matsushita, 1991

31 (d) Bill Vukovich III

32 (b) Mark Donohue

33 (b) Nashville, MI

34 (b) Joe Leonard

35 (c) George Mack, 2002

36 (d) Rodger Ward

37 (a) Belgium

38 (b) Jim Hurtubise

39 (c) Coffeyville, KS

40 (b) Gaston Chevrolet

41 (c) four years

42 (b) Parsippany, NJ

43 (a) the Andrettis—Mario, Michael, Jeff, and John (father, son, son, and nephew/cousin)

44 (b) Jan

45 (a) Gary Bettenhausen

46 (c) Eddie Sachs

47 (c) Ray Keech, 1929

48 (d) Wichita Falls, TX

49 (c) Daniel

50 (c) Danny Ongais

51 (d) Rufus

52 (a) Peter DePaolo

53 (d) four

54 (d) 52

55 Mario Andretti: (a) Nazareth, PA

Gary Bettenhausen: (d) Tinley Park, IL

Len Sutton: (c) Portland, OR

Chip Ganassi: (b) Pittsburgh, PA

Roger McCluskey: (e) Tucson, AZ

56 (c) Josele Garza

57 (a) Tommy Milton

58 (d) Lee Wallard

59 (a) Brown University

60 (c) Troy Ruttman

61 (a) Peter DePaolo

(c) Jimmy Murphy

62 (c) Teddy Pilette, 1977—He did not qualify. His grandfather Theodore finished fifth in 1913.

63 (b) Dick Rathmann

64 (b) Danny Ongais

65 (d) Al and Al Unser Jr.

66 (b) Hastings, MI

67 (a) Australia

68 (d) Rodger Ward

69 (a) Jimmy Caruthers

70 (d) Carl Scarborough

71 (c) French

72 (a) Denison

73 (c) 45

74 (d) taxicab driver

75 (b) Chet Fillip

76 (b) Rick Mears

77 (a) 19 years old

78 (d) Whittington family, 1982: Bill, Don, and Dale

79 (c) Chris Kneifel

80 (a) Patrick Bedard

81 (d) Howdy Holmes

82 (b) Al Unser Sr., 1970, 1971

83 (c) snow skiing

84 (c) Al Unser III

85 (a) Michael Andretti

86 (b) 1993

87 (d) Purdue University

88 (c) Roscoe, Illinois

89 (a) Helio Castroneves

90 (a) Paul Dana

91 (c) Bob Sweikert

92 (d) Dan Wheldon, 2005

93 (c) not related

94 (b) no appearance money offered

95 (d) Tora Takagi, 2003—fifth place

96 (a) the Bedouin

97 (c) North Vernon, IN

98 (a) blistered hands

99 (b) Leon Duray Sirois

100 (b) Hollywood stuntman

101 (a) George Stewart

102 (a) airplane crash

103 (c) insurance company executive

104 (c) 55

105 (d) assistant high school principal

106 (d) tavern

107 (d) Eddie Sachs

108 (d) Tim Richmond

109 (d) roller-skating rink

110 (b) Mad Russian

111 (d) Greg Ray

112 (d) Bud Tinglestad

113 (d) Danica Patrick, 2005—fourth place

   (e) Lyn St. James, 1992—11th place

114 (c) Walt Hansgen

115 (b) Lloyd Ruby

116 (f) #8

117 (b) 1973

118 (b) Jim Hurtubise

119 (b) Louis Meyer

120 (d) Bill Puterbaugh, 1975

121 (b) Jiffy Mix

122 (b) Clark

123 (a) #56

Chapter 2: Track/Facility

124 (a) 1914

125 (d) The Old Pressley Farm

126 (a) nine degrees and 12 minutes

127 (b) 1976

128 (c) 1976

129 (b) 1968

130 (b) 1972

131 (c) 1956

132 (b) $220,000

133 (c) Tony George

134 (d) 1962

135 (d) motorcycle race

136 (a) $700,000

137 (c) 3,200,000 at 13 cents each

138 (b) 30 years old

139 (a) 1956

140 (b) one—George Barringer's

141 (c) 2000

142 (a) 1957

143 corners: (b) 1/4 mile

short chutes: (a) 1/8 mile

straights: (c) 5/8 mile

144 (c) 1971

145 (b) Carl Fisher

146 (b) $700,000

147 (c) 1967

148 (d) Bill Vandewater

149 (b) Homer Cochran

150 (b) balloon race

151 (d) 1985

152 (b) 1929

153 (a) 1935

154 James Allison: (b) 1923–1927

Joie Chitwood III: (j) 2004–2009

Joe Cloutier, first tenure: (f) 1977–1979

Joe Cloutier, second tenure: (h) 1982–1989

John Cooper: (g) 1979–1982

Carl Fisher: (a) 1909–1923

Tony George: (i) 1989–2004

Tony Hulman: (e) 1954–1977

Eddie Rickenbacker: (c) 1927–1945

Wilbur Shaw: (d) 1945–1954

155 (d) 1973

156 (c) Miami Beach

157 (a) 63 days

158 (b) Eastern Airlines

159 (b) Sid Collins

160 (b) 1962

161 (b) 1974

162 (b) 1959

163 (c) 1993

164 (c) 1950

165 Brian Howard: (f) 1997–present

Seth Klein: (a) 1925–1927

Seth Klein: (b) 1934–1953

Duane Sweeney: (e) 1980–1996

Bill Vandewater: (c) 1954–1961

Pat Vidan: (d) 1962–1979

166 (d) Stark and Wetzel

167 (c) 1957

168 (d) Wilbur Shaw

169 (b) Clabber Girl Corporation

170 (c) 1946

171 Brian Barnhart: (j) 1998–present

Tom Binford: (h) 1974–1995

Ted Doescher: (c) 1940–1941

Eddie Edenburn: (a) 1919–1934

Harlan Fengler: (g) 1958–1973

Harry McQuinn: (f) 1953–1957

Jack Mehan: (d) 1946–1948

Charlie Merz: (b) 1935–1939

Tommy Milton: (e) 1949–1952

Keith Ward: (i) 1996–1997

172 (b) 1947

173 (c) 50 feet

174 (b) 1921

175 (a) James Allison

(b) Carl Fisher

(e) Arthur Newby

(i) Frank Wheeler

176 (a) 1936

177 (a) airplane crash

178 (b) 60 feet

179 (b) 1935

180 (a) 1936

181 (c) 1957

182 (d) Yale

Chapter 3: Owners/Teams

183 (b) Andy, Joe and Vince Granatelli

184 (b) 1969

185 (d) Jim Trueman

186 (a) Ganassi Racing

187 (d) Team Scandia—seven cars in 1996

(Zampedri, Gosek, Salazar, Alboreto

Jourdain, Gardner, Velez)

188 (d) Bobby Unser

189 (d) Evil Knievel

190 (d) Treadway Racing—Luyendyk and Goodyear

191 (a) Ted Field

192 (a) A. J. Foyt, 1958

193 (c) Spike Jones

194 (d) scientifically treated petroleum

195 (d) Lou Moore, five wins

(1938, 1941, 1947, 1948, and 1949)

196 (a) Andy Granatelli

197 (a) Chip Ganassi

198 (c) Mike Groff

199 (b) Bobby Johns

200 (b) Ebb Rose

201 (a) Mike Hiss

202 (b) Phil Hedback

203 (d) Penske Racing—Rick Mears, Danny Sullivan, Al Unser Sr.

204 (a) George Bignotti

205 (d) Simon Racing

206 (a) Castroneves/de Ferran, 2001

207 (d) Harry Miller

208 (a) wrest on their laurels and cease their racing program

209 (d) 11

210 (c) Lindsey Hopkins

211 (c) McLaren

Chapter 4: Race Information

212 (a) Marco Andretti

213 (b) Mary Fendrich Hulman

214 (c) Diane Hunt

215 (b) Sam Hornish Jr.

216 (d) two-lap penalty for passing pace car

217 (c) 189

218 (d) Tomas Scheckter

219 Les Anderson: (b) 11th, 1947

George Barringer: (a) eighth, 1936

Bill Cantrell: (d) 21st, 1949

Joie Chitwood: (c) 15th, 1940

220 (c) Rick Mears

221 (b) Roberto Guerrero

222 (c) 190

223 (b) Jim Malloy

224 (b) two times

225 1926: (d) 160 laps

1950: (c) 138 laps

1973: (b) 133 laps

1975: (f) 174 laps

1976: (a) 102 laps

2004: (g) 180 laps

2007: (e) 166 laps

226 (a) Larry "Boom Boom" Cannon

227 (c) Bill Holland

228 (c) 400 miles

229 Spike Gelhausen: (b) Jasper, IN

Parnelli Jones: (e) Torrance, CA

Pete Halsmer: (c) Lafayette, IN

Mel Kenyon: (d) Lebanon, IN

Sheldon Kinser: (a) Bloomington, IN

230 Sid Collins: (a) 1952–1976

Bob Jenkins: (d) 1990–1998

Mike King: (e) 1999–present

Paul Page: (b) 1977–1987

Lou Palmer: (c) 1988–1989

231 (a) Wally Dallenbach

232 (d) five (row one: pace car and four cars; last row: one car)

233 (a) Joe Boyer

234 (d) Wood Brothers

235 (b) 1967

236 (b) Gary Bettenhausen

237 (d) 195 laps

238 (c) Hector Rebaque

239 (a) Ryan Briscoe

240 (d) Lee Wallard, 1951

241 (b) Davey Hamilton

242 (a) Billy Arnold (riding mechanic: Spider Matlock)

243 (d) 185

244 (c) Tom Sneva

245 (b) 174

246 (d) lap 197

247 (d) 192 laps

248 (d) 190

249 Billy Arnold, 1930: (d) 198

Jim Clark, 1965: (a or b) 190

Al Unser, 1970: (a or b) 190

Bill Vukovich, 1953: (c) 195

250 (d) orange juice

251 (c) 80,000

252 (b) 1940

253 (b) 1920

254 (c) three

255 (b) Ralph Hepburn

256 (c) Jaques Lazier

257 (a) Alabama

258 (b) 1936

259 (b) Mario Andretti

260 (a) 1946

261 (c) 11

262 (d) 2006—Hornish passed Marco Andretti

263 (c) 29

264 (b) Roberto Guerrero

265 (c) Wilbur Shaw, 1941

266 (d) 197

267 (d) lap 197

268 (d) milk (buttermilk)

269 (d) to retire from racing

270 (b) Foyt (Larry: 32nd; A .J. IV: 33rd)

271 (a) back fractures

272 (a) Johnny Boyd

273 (c) Jackie Stewart (*Louis Meyer drove relief in 1927 before winning in 1928 in his first start.)

274 (b) six years—1917, 1918, 1942, 1943, 1944, 1945

275 (c) Johnny Rutherford, 1976

276 (d) Bobby Unser, 1981

277 (c) Troy Ruttman

278 (b) Robby Gordon

279 (c) $14,250

280 (a) Bobby Allison

281 (a) 0.16 seconds

282 (d) Tim Richmond

283 (a) 1949

284 (a) champagne

285 (a) Mario Andretti

286 (c) 1986

287 (c) Louis Meyer

288 (b) one

289 (d) 196—from lap three to lap 198

290 (c) broken wrist

291 (d) Paul Tracy

292 (b) 193

293 (a) 133 laps

294 (c) 1948

295 (c) Mauri Rose

296 (c) Vitor Meira

297 (a) Ed Elisian

298 (d) Dennis Vitolo

299 (c) Floyd Roberts

    (d) Bill Vukovich

300 (b) Pat Flaherty

301 (c) 170 laps

302 (d) Eldon Rasmussen

303 (d) six laps

304 (d) Cyrus Patchke

305 (d) five cars – Zampedri, Schmidt, Brack, Giaffone, Gregoire

306 (b) 1940

307 (c) Saturday

308 (b) Buddy Lazier

309 (c) fourth

310 (a) Norm Batten

311 (d) 180

312 (c) rookies won the race in successive years.

313 (b) 184

314 (d) J. J. Yeley

315 (d) Lee Roy Yarbrough

316 (c) gearbox

317 (c) Art Pollard

318 (a) 13

319 (d) Wednesday

320 (c) Arie Luyendyk

321 (c) Bobby Rahal, 1986

322 (b) A. J. Foyt

323 (c) Roberto Guerrero

324 (c) blistered tires

325 (a) Eddie Cheever

326 (c) Dick Simon

327 (a) added more fuel than necessary to finish

328 (d) 191

329 (d) Gordon Johncock

330 (d) 1982

331 (b) Davy Jones

332 (c) 191

333 (c) Gil de Ferran

334 (a) 1949

335 (d) eight years

336 (d) Jerry Unser

337 (b) four tires

338 (a) Eddie Cheever

339 (c) hot dog

340 (a) Duane Carter Sr.

     (c) Eddie Johnson

     (f) Rodger Ward

341 (c) 1988

342 (b) Tony Hulman

343 (b) Cliff Bergere

344 (b) Bill Fox, sports editor Indianapolis News

345 (d) Salt Walther

346 (b) Dan Gurney

347 (b) bottomed out, ripping out oil plug

348 (c) Johnnie Parsons—misspelled as Johnny Parsons

Chapter 5: Cars/Engines

349 (c) Jigger Sirois

350 (c) broken fuel shaft

351 (d) Offenhauser

352 (c) a place in Michigan

353 (c) four

354 (d) Rachel's Potato Chips

355 (b) green

356 (b) Silent Sam

(d) Whooshmobile

357 1963: (e) #92

1964: (a) #6

1965: (d) #82

1966: (b) #19

1967: (c) #31

358 (b) Duesenberg, with a Miller engine

359 (c) 1930, Billy Arnold

360 (c) 1948

361 (a) Allen Crowe

362 (c) third

363 (a) 1937

364 (c) six wheels

365 (b) Joe Leonard

366 (b) Art Malone

367 (d) 1963, Jim Clark and Dan Gurney—Ford Lotus

368 (c) #32

369 (c) 1949, Bill Holland

370 (c) Al Unser Sr.

371 (c) pink

372 (d) Bruce Walkup

373 (d) twin engines—one in front of the driver and one behind the driver

374 (a) Duane Carter

375 (b) Cliff Griffith

376 (c) seven

377 (a) Colt

378 (c) McNamara

379 (d) Sunoco

380 (c) Honda

381 (d) Yellow Submarine

382 (a) one

383 (c) Danny Ongais

384 (c) Skoal Bandit

385 (c) 900

386 (d) rookie driver

387 (a) Jimmy Bryan

388 (a) foreign-built

389 (c) Maurice Phillipe

390 (b) France

391 (b) Maserati

392 (d) Lou Welch

393 (a) Bobby Grim

394 (a) doorstops

395 (a) dinosaur

396 (c) tropical rose and cream

397 (d) Bill Vukovich II

398 (c) ninth

399 (d) #68

400 (b) Graham Hill

Chapter 6: Rules and Regulations

401 (b) 1934

402 (d) 1990

403 (c) red

404 (b) 1959

405 (d) 1946

406 (b) 1933

407 (c) 1957

408 (a) 1935

409 (a) 37.5 gallons

410 (c) 1956

411 (a) 1921

412 (c) 1956

413 (b) 1979

414 (b) Jerry Grant

415 (c) 1965

416 (c) 40 gallons

417 (d) Louis Schneider

418 (c) 1973

419 (c) red hat

420 (d) 400 feet

421 (b) 1937

422 (c) 350 miles

423 (b) rookie tests for all new drivers

424 (a) Magnaflux

425 (a) 1915

426 (b) "junk" era

427 (d) 1963

428 (a) three miles

429 (b) 1939

Chapter 7: Qualifications

430 (a) Scott Brayton

431 Milka Duno: (e) 27th

    Sarah Fisher: (c) ninth

    Janet Guthrie: (d) 14th

    Danica Patrick: (a) fourth

    Lyn St. James: (b) sixth

432 (d) Jigger Sirois

433 (a) second (1984)

434 (b) Teo Fabi

435 (c) six times

436 (c) Penske Racing

437 (b) Billy Devore (Earl Devore: second, 1927; Billy Devore: seventh, 1937)

438 (a) fifth—never better than 16th in three previous races

439 (b) sixth

440 (a) fourth—never better than 16th in three previous races

441 (b) 25th

442 (c) 1968

443 (a) first

  (b) second

  (c) third

  (e) fifth

  (d) fourth

444 (d) George Snider

445 (b) Buddy Lazier

446 (b) 35 cars

447 (c) Len Sutton

448 (d) Johnny Rutherford

449 (a) Gary Bettenhausen

450 (c) ten laps

Chapter 8: Records

451 (c) 1971

452 (d) Bill Vukovich—1953, 1954

453 (b) Louis Meyer—1928, 1933, and also 1936

454 (c) Mari Hulman George

455 (d) 61

456 (d) Bobby Unser

457 (d) Arie Luyendyk

458 Mario Andretti: (b) 556

Ralph DePalma: (c) 612

A. J. Foyt: (a) 555

Al Unser Sr. (d): 644

459 Unser Jr. and Goodyear: (a) 0.0430

De ferran and Castroneves: (d) 0.2990

Johncock and Mears: (c) 0.1600

Hornish and Andretti: (b) 0.0635

460 (d) Billy Arnold, 1930

461 (c) 35

462 (d) Al Unser Sr. (1987)

463 (a) Buzz Calkins

464 (b) Mauri Rose—1941, 1947, 1948

465 (c) A. J. Foyt

466 (c) 1930

467 (b) Scott Dixon

468 (a) A. J. Foyt

469 (a) George Bailey, 1939

470 (c) 186 mph

471 (b) Peter DePaolo, 1925

472 (d) five—Art Cross, Johnnie Parsons, Sam Hanks, Andy Linden, and Jimmy Davies

473 (d) Troy Ruttman

474 (d) Bobby and Al Unser

475 (c) $3,048,005

476 (a) Mario Andretti

477 (d) He completed the race without a pit stop.

478 (b) Buddy Lazier (father: Bob Lazier, 1981)

 (c) Al Unser Jr. (father: Al Unser Sr., 27 starts)

479 (b) 1952

480 (c) 52

481 (a) Ted Horn

482 (b) Janet Guthrie, 1977

483 (a) Don Branson, at Phoenix

484 (c) Lyn St. James

485 (b) Tommy Milton—1921 and 1923

486 (c) Jim McElreath

487 (c) 75 mph

488 (b) Larry Bisceglia

489 (a) Louis Meyer—1928, 1933, and 1936

490 (d) 117

491 (d) Juan Pablo Montoya

492 Fred Frame, 1932: (b) 27th

 Ray Harroun, 1911: (c or d) 28th

Louis Meyer, 1936: (c or d) 28th

Johnny Rutherford, 1974: (a) 25th

493 (b) 1967

494 (b) 1964

495 (d) ten of 13 races

496 (c) Parnelli Jones

497 (a) 21

498 (c) Jack McGrath

499 (b) Arlene Hiss—1976 season opener at Phoenix

500 (d) Tom Sneva

501 (b) six mph

502 (c) Al Unser Sr.—1970, 1971, 1978, and 1987

503 (c) 1952

504 (c) Jim and James McElreath, in 1977

505 (b) Sam Hanks, 1957

506 (a) first alternate starter (qualifier "Uncle" Jacques
     Villeneuve was injured)

507 (d) 1976, 102 laps

508 (b) 1953

509 (a) 1916

510 (d) 17

511 (d) Al Unser

512 (a) 92 laps

513 (d) Jacques Villeneuve

514 (a) John Andretti

515 (d) Lou Moore—1947, 1948, and 1949

516 (a) Helio Castroneves

517 (b) Art Cross

518 (c) Elaine Irwin-Mellencamp, 2001

519 (c) Wilbur Shaw

520 (b) Ted Horn

521 (a) Johnny Aitken

522 (b) Jules Goux, 1913

523 (c) 1933

524 (a) 45 gallons

525 (b) Jimmy Clark

526 (b) six times

1911: Ray Harroun/Cyrus Patschke (about one hour)

1912: Joe Dawson/Don Herr (laps 108–144)

1923: Tommy Milton/Howdy Wilcox (laps 103–151)

1924: L. L. Corum/Joe Boyer (laps 111–200)

1925: Peter DePaolo/Norm Batten (about 35 minutes)

1941: Floyd Davis/Mauri Rose (laps 72–200)

527 (d) Tony Kanaan

528 (c) Jules Goux, 1913

529 (a) Andretti

Chapter 9 - Green/White/Checker

530 Joe Dawson (b) Don Herr

Peter DePaolo (a) Norm Batten

Ray Harroun (c) Cyrus Patschke

Tommy Milton (d) Howdy Wilcox

531 (c) Karl Kizer

532 (c) Pelican Joe

533 (b) Lora Corum

(c) Floyd Davis

534 (d) Eddie Sachs

535 (d) Johnnie Parsons

536 Mario Andretti (a) Two

Jim Clark (h) 82

Mark Donohue (g) 66

Graham Hill (e) 24

Gordon Johncock (d) 20

Buddy Lazier (i) 91

Troy Ruttman (j) 98

Tom Sneva (b) Five

Jacques Villeneuve (f) 27

Bill Vukovich (c) 14

537 (c) Herm Johnson

538 (a) 1916 (Johnny Aitken)

539 (d) 1946

540 (c) Harry Hartz

541 (c) 1949

542 (d) 1960

543 (b) Art Cross

544 (b) Jerry Hoyt

545 (b) George

546 (c) 38 years old

547 (c) Bobby Johns

548 (d) Greg Weld

549 (c) Al Retzloff

550 (c) Gordon Johncock

551 (a) Wally Dallenbach

552 (d) Jan Opperman

553 (c) John Martin

554 (a) Bill Alsup

555 (b) Rick Mears

556 (d) Travelon Trailer

557 (c) 1979

558 (c) Rex Mays 22 years and 81 days (1935)

559 (a) Cliff Bergere 49 years and 175 days (1946)

560 Jim Clark (c) 160

Roberto Guerrero (j) 230

Graham Hill (d) 170

Parnelli Jones (b) 150

Jack McGrath (a) 140

Rick Mears (i) 220

Tom Sneva (g) 200

Tom Sneva (h) 210

Bobby Unser (f) 190

Bill Vukovich Jr. (e) 180

561 (d) Rick Mears (1986-1991)

562 (b) Dan Gurney

563 (b) 1974

564 (d) 1963

565 (c) Dan Gurney

566 (c) Al Unser Sr. (1970-1987)

567 Gaston Chevrolet (e) 14 laps

Joe Dawson (a) two laps

Mark Donohue (d) 13 laps

Graham Hill (b) ten laps

Bobby Unser (1975) (c) 11 laps

Jacques Villeneuve (f) 15 laps

568 (a) Eloise "Dolly" Dallenbach

569 (d) Wilbur Shaw

570 (d) Tommy Milton

571 (b) Chickie Hirashima

572 (c) John Cooper

573 (a) aerospace engineer

574 (c) 1972

575 (c) Josele Garza

576 (c) 1982

577 (a) Fabrizio Barbazza

578 (a) Eric Bachelart

579 (c) Robby Gordon

580 (b) Andy Hillenburg

581 (c) Laurent Redon

Arie Luyendyk set the fastest official lap in track history at 237.498 mph in 1996 qualifications.

Chapter 11
Grading

1: Drivers	_____	out of 123
2: Track/Facility	_____	out of 59
3: Owners/Teams	_____	out of 29
4: Race Information	_____	out of 137
5: Cars/Engines	_____	out of 52
6: Rules and Regulations	_____	out of 29
7: Qualifications	_____	out of 21
8: Records	_____	out of 79
9: Green/White/Checker	_____	out of 52
Total	_____	out of 581

Answers Correct:

0–100   Did not make the race

101–150   Rookie

151–250   Race participant

251–300   One-time winner

301–350   Two-time winner (Tommy Milton, Bill Vukovich, Rodger Ward, Gordon Johncock, Emerson Fittipaldi, Al Unser Jr., Arie Luyendyk and Dario Franchitti)

351–400   Three-time winner (Louis Meyer, Wilbur Shaw, Mauri Rose, Johnny Rutherford, Bobby Unser, and Helio Castroneves)

401–500   Four-time winner (A. J. Foyt, Al Unser Sr., and Rick Mears)

501 and Above   Donald Davidson

In 2009, Helio Castroneves captures his third Indy
500 win and Roger Penske's 15th car-owner victory.

Resources

Bloemker, Al. 500 Miles to Go.

Davidson, Donald, and Rick Shaffer. The Official History of the Indianapolis 500.

Devaney, John and Barbara. The Indianapolis 500.

Engel, Lyle Kenyon. Mario Andretti - The Man Who Can Win Any Kind of Race

Granatelli, Andy. They Call Me Mister 500.

Indianapolis 500: The Legacy Series (video collection)

Kramer, Ralph. Indianapolis 500 – A Century of Excitement

Kramer, Ralph. Indianapolis Motor Speedway: 100 Years of Racing.

Shaw, Wilbur. Gentlemen, Start Your Engines.

Pictures courtesy of the Indianapolis Motor Speedway

About the Author

Pat Kennedy attended his first Indianapolis 500 with his family in 1963 when he was six years old. He has not missed a race since. His interest and passion was immediate and has continued to grow, culminating in this collection.

His grandfather and father sponsored race cars at Indy from 1936 to the early 1950s under the name of their family-owned business: the Kennedy Tank Special. Kennedy Tank and Manufacturing Company has been a supplier of pit fueling tanks for many years at Indy. Pat has continued the family tradition of involvement in the Indy 500.

Pat is the president of a group of family-owned companies, including Kennedy Tank and Manufacturing Company (Indianapolis, IN); Southern Tank and Manufacturing Company (Owensboro, KY), and Steel Tank and Fabricating Corp., (Columbia City, IN).

www.autoracingtrivia.com

CPSIA information can be obtained at www.ICGtesting.com

261136BV00001B/2/P